TABLE OF CONTENTS

I0878284

Top 15 Test Taking Tips

1. Know the test directions, duration, topics, question types, how many questions
2. Setup a flexible study schedule at least 3-4 weeks before test day
3. Study during the time of day you are most alert, relaxed, and stress free
4. Maximize your learning style; visual learner use visual study aids, auditory learner use auditory study aids
5. Focus on your weakest knowledge base
6. Find a study partner to review with and help clarify questions
7. Practice, practice, practice
8. Get a good night's sleep; don't try to cram the night before the test
9. Eat a well balanced meal
10. Wear comfortable, loose fitting, layered clothing; prepare for it to be either cold or hot during the test
11. Eliminate the obviously wrong answer choices, then guess the first remaining choice
12. Pace yourself; don't rush, but keep working and move on if you get stuck
13. Maintain a positive attitude even if the test is going poorly
14. Keep your first answer unless you are positive it is wrong
15. Check your work, don't make a careless mistake

Chapter 1 - Place Value and Number Sense

Lesson 1

Finding Patterns

Draw the shape that comes next in the pattern.

1. 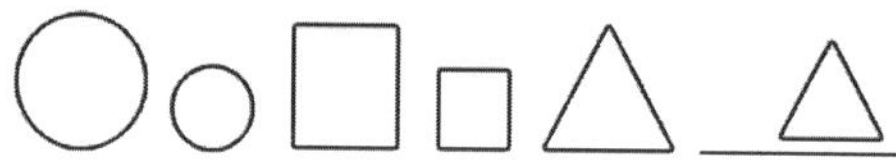 ______

2. 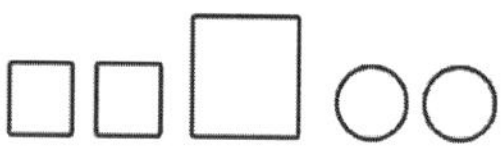 ______

3. 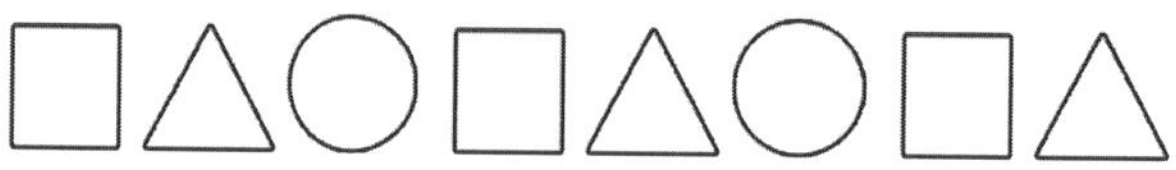 ______

4. 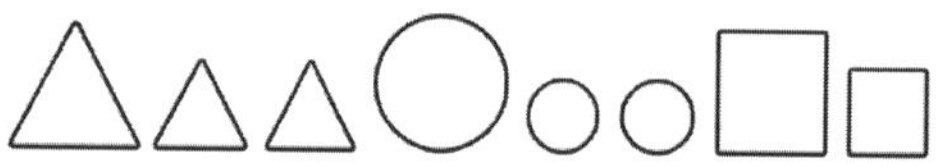 ______

5. 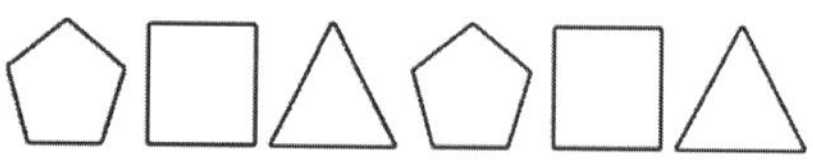 ______

6. 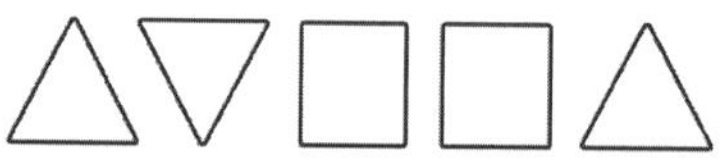 ______

7. 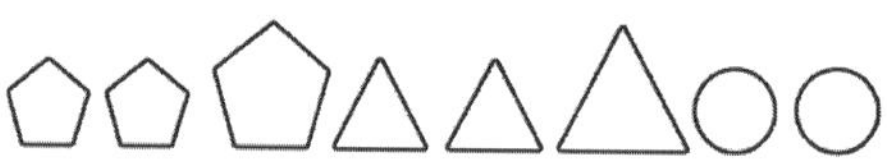 ______

8. 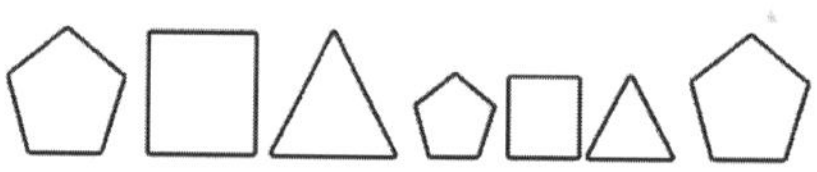 ______

Lesson 2

Even and Odd Numbers 1

Even numbers are any number that can be divided exactly by 2.

Odd numbers are any number that can not be divided exactly by 2.

Are these numbers even or odd? Answer each question.

1. 4 even

2. 5 ________

3. 6 ________

4. 8 ________

5. 15 ________

6. 26 ________

7. 33 ________

8. 45 ________

9. 8 ________

10. 9 ________

11. 17 ________

12. 16 ________

13. 75 ________

14. 50 ________

15. 10 ________

16. 2 ________

17. 61 ________

18. 77 ________

19. 40 ________

20. 14 ________

21. 31 ________

22. 99 ________

23. 80 ________

24. 100 ________

Even and Odd Numbers 2

Even numbers are any number that can be divided exactly by 2.

Odd numbers are any number that can not be divided exactly by 2.

Are these numbers even or odd? Answer each question.

1. 121 ___odd___

2. 200 ________

3. 324 ________

4. 175 ________

5. 91 ________

6. 568 ________

7. 963 ________

8. 828 ________

9. 500 ________

10. 24 ________

11. 753 ________

12. 333 ________

13. 300 ________

14. 211 ________

15. 771 ________

16. 84 ________

17. 140 ________

18. 508 ________

19. 64 ________

20. 262 ________

21. 257 ________

22. 443 ________

23. 29 ________

24. 266 ________

Lesson 3

Rounding to the nearest 100

Round the following numbers to the nearest hundred.

1. 285 300

2. 863 ______

3. 262 ______

4. 83 ______

5. 211 ______

6. 819 ______

7. 828 ______

8. 144 ______

9. 751 ______

10. 373 ______

11. 305 ______

12. 267 ______

13. 611 ______

14. 996 ______

15. 150 ______

16. 326 ______

17. 356 ______

18. 704 ______

19. 740 ______

20. 508 ______

21. 164 ______

22. 771 ______

23. 266 ______

24. 238 ______

25. 753 ______

26. 194 ______

27. 789 ______

28. 333 ______

Lesson 4

Rounding to the nearest 1000

Round the following numbers to the nearest thousand.

1. 7,998 8,000

2. 998 ______

3. 2,342 ______

4. 8,623 ______

5. 1,456 ______

6. 5,946 ______

7. 3,732 ______

8. 9,258 ______

9. 1,925 ______

10. 6,987 ______

11. 2,229 ______

12. 4,589 ______

13. 6,872 ______

14. 3,549 ______

15. 7,100 ______

16. 8,596 ______

17. 1,329 ______

18 4,879 ______

19. 5,038 ______

20. 1,589 ______

21. 2,338 ______

22. 915 ______

23. 1,598 ______

24. 4,928 ______

25. 1,275 ______

26. 8,615 ______

27. 7,589 ______

28. 3,333 ______

Lesson 5

Finding Patterns

Figure out what the numbers in each row have in common. Circle the number in each row that doesn't belong.

1. 10 20 30 78 50 60
2. 5 10 34 20 25 30
3. 2 4 15 8 10 12
4. 8 2 24 32 40 48
5. 3 5 7 8 9 11
6. 50 60 9 80 90 100
7. 55 65 75 85 95 3
8. 5 8 10 12 14 16
9. 3 5 7 9 11 89

Lesson 6

Place Value by 10's

All two digit whole numbers have a tens and a ones place.

Tens Ones

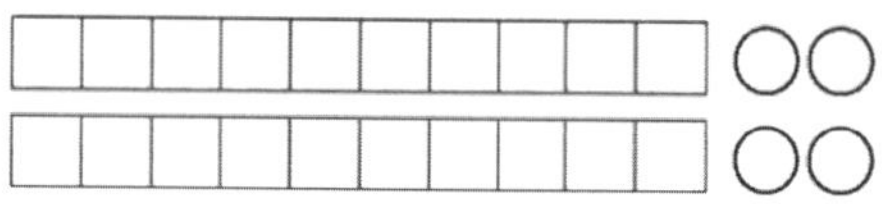

= Tens | Ones: 2 | 4 = 24

Count the groups, then write the numbers.

1. 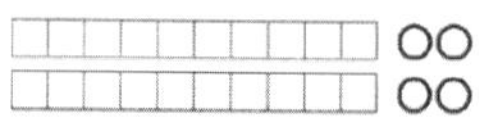 = 24

2. 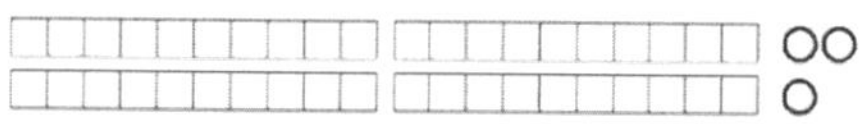 = ______

3. 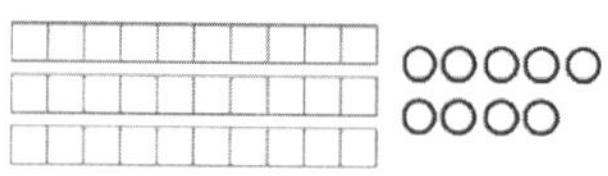 = ______

4. 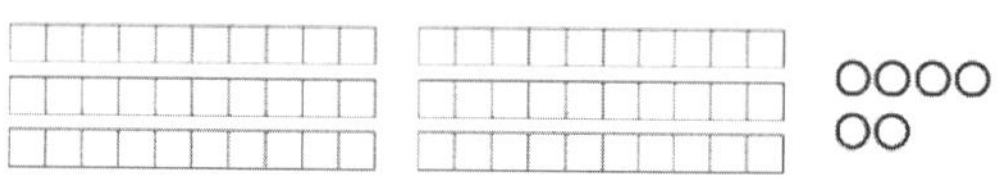 = ______

5. 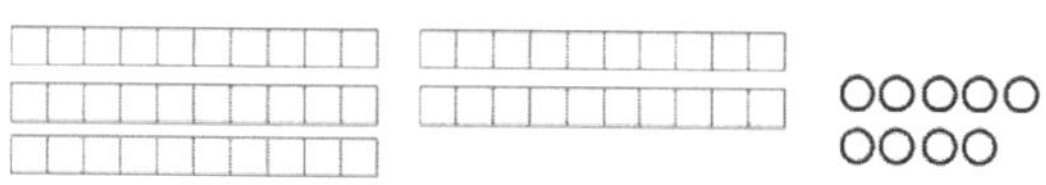 = ______

6. 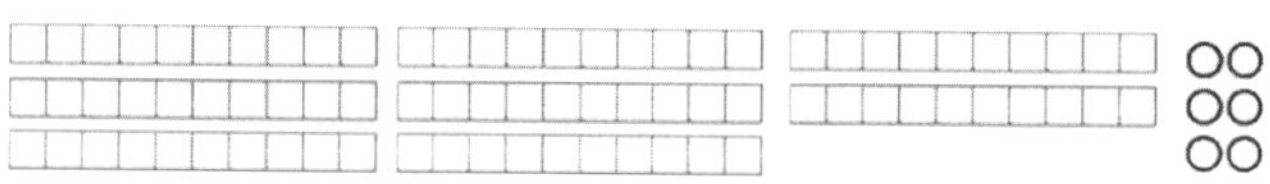 = ______

Lesson 7

Place Value by 100's

All three digit whole numbers have a hundreds, tens and a ones place.

Hundreds Tens Ones

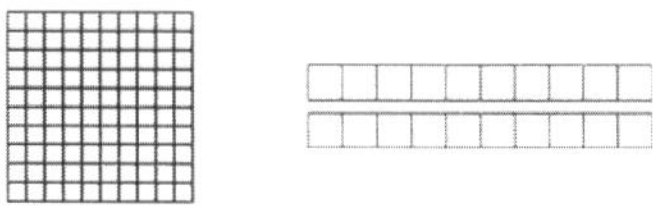

OO
OO

=

Hundreds	Tens	Ones
1	2	4

= 124

Count the groups, then write the numbers.

1. 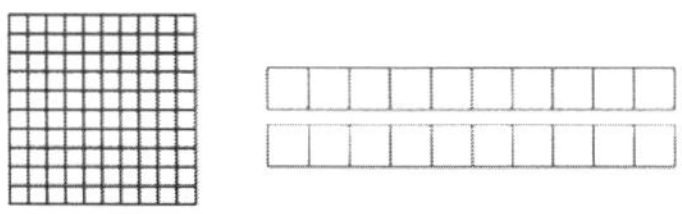 OOOOO OOOO = 129

2. 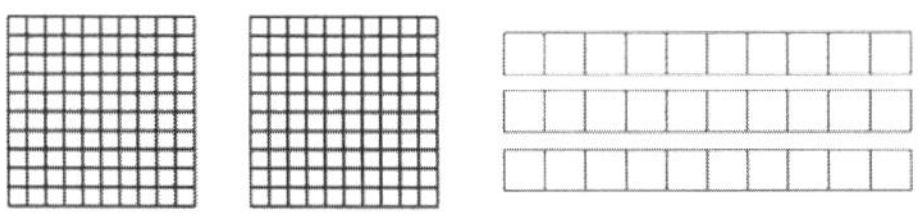 OOO OO = ______

3. 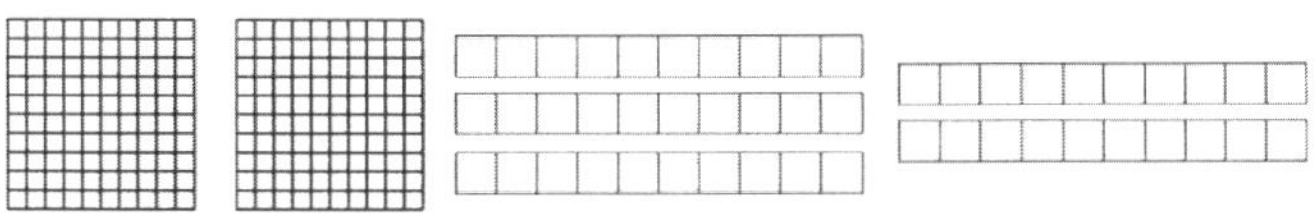 OO OO = ______

4. 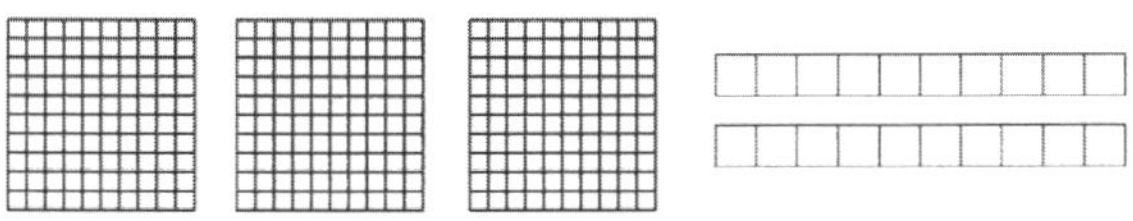 OOO OO = ______

5. 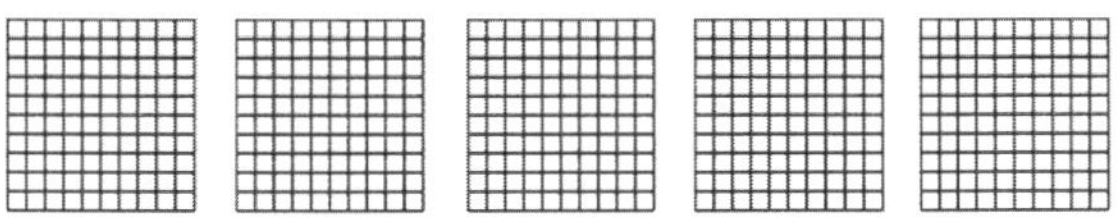 OOOO OOO = ______

Lesson 8

Place Value by 1000's

All four digit whole numbers have a thousands, hundreds, tens and a ones place.

Thousands Hundreds Tens Ones

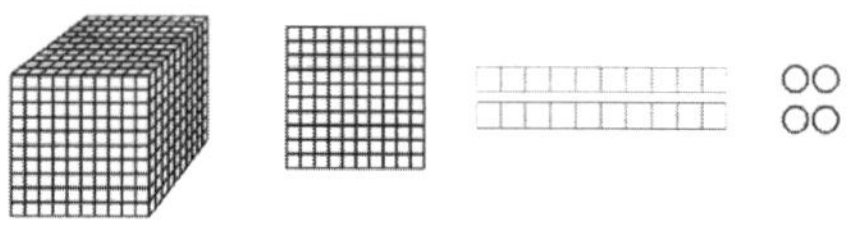

=

Thousands	Hundreds	Tens	Ones
1	1	2	4

= 1,124

Count the groups, then write the numbers.

1. 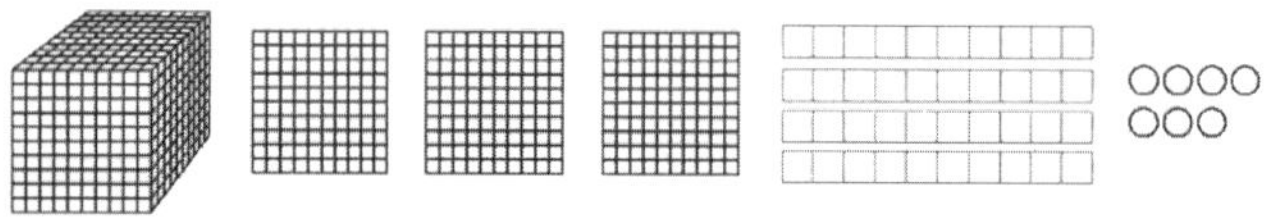 = 1,347

2. 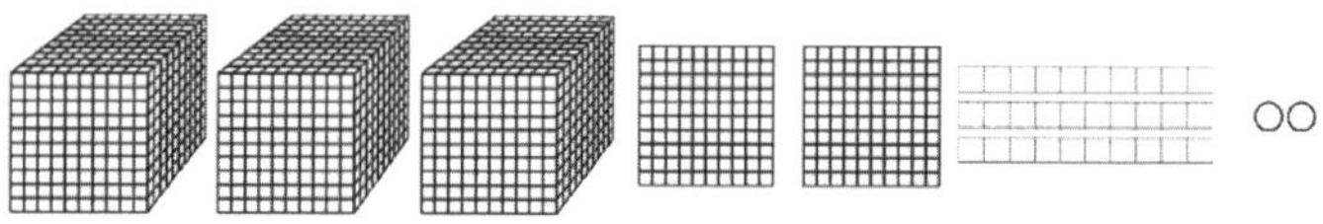 = ______

3. 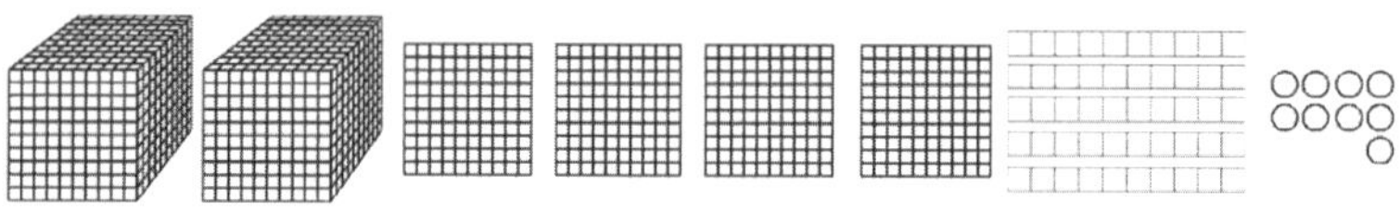 = ______

4. 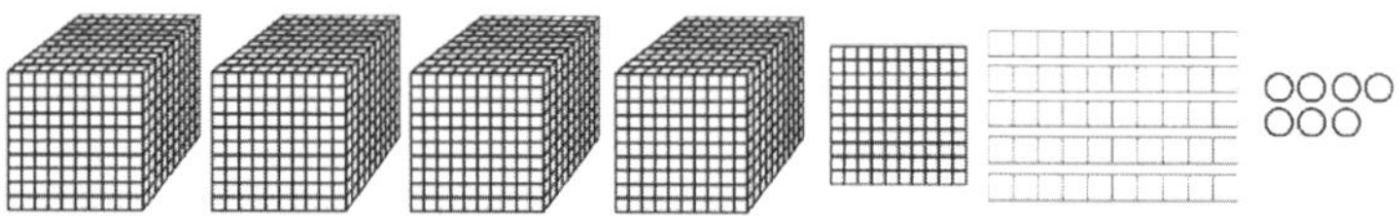 = ______

5. 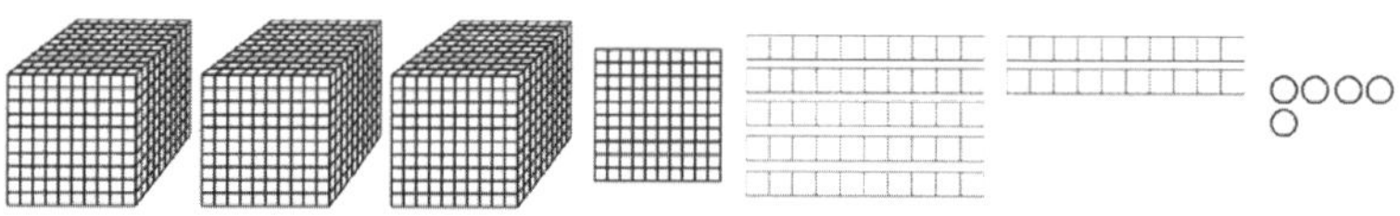 = ______

Lesson 9

Least to Greatest

Write these numbers from least to greatest.

1. 4,982 4,818 14,818 4,818, 4,982, 14,818

2. 1,900 880 1,251 ____________________

3. 1,541 1,210 1,780 ____________________

4. 129 74 50 ____________________

5. 3,500 815 1,520 ____________________

6. 5,800 3,400 9,570 ____________________

7. 100 1,000 10 ____________________

8. 4,500 5 330 ____________________

9. 250 275 300 ____________________

10. 54 25 16 ____________________

Lesson 10

Comparing Numbers 1

Compare the numbers. Write >,<, or = for each question.

1. 561 [>] 350
2. 1,234 [ ] 999
3. 3,500 [ ] 3,589
4. 85 [ ] 100
5. 5,329 [ ] 5,579
6. 1,050 [ ] 1,050
7. 28 [ ] 28
8. 674 [ ] 700
9. 2,300 [ ] 1,949
10. 2,012 [ ] 2,430
11. 4,259 [ ] 1,742
12. 330 [ ] 6,821
13. 4,120 [ ] 559
14. 165 [ ] 165
15. 50 [ ] 32
16. 832 [ ] 540
17. 1,100 [ ] 1,200
18. 2,180 [ ] 2,180
19. 6,432 [ ] 6,438
20. 2,451 [ ] 2,680

Comparing Numbers 2

Compare the numbers. Write >,<, or = for each question.

1. 2,432 > 1,684
2. 2,100 ☐ 4,681
3. 3.210 ☐ 3,210
4. 5,541 ☐ 3,210
5. 4,850 ☐ 4,000
6. 1,329 ☐ 1,150
7. 540 ☐ 1,050
8. 3,167 ☐ 4,502
9. 33 ☐ 33
10. 48 ☐ 65
11. 1,982 ☐ 1,090
12. 1,500 ☐ 1,800
13. 6,780 ☐ 2,500
14. 280 ☐ 280
15. 451 ☐ 842
16. 1,100 ☐ 2,781
17. 999 ☐ 999
18. 8,671 ☐ 5,672
19. 2,050 ☐ 2,000
20. 300 ☐ 700

Lesson 11

Converting Symbols to Numbers

Each shape equals a number on the chart.

⬠	□	△	○
1,000	100	10	1

Use the chart and shapes to write each number.

1. ⬠□□△△○ 1,221
2. ⬠⬠□△△△△○○ ______
3. □□□△△△○○○ ______
4. ⬠⬠⬠□□□△△○ ______
5. ⬠⬠□□□△△△△ ______

Lesson 12

Place Value up to 100,000

The place value of a digit is determined by where it is in a number.

Hundred Thousands	Ten Thousands	Thousands	Hundreds	Tens	Ones
1	2	3	4	5	6

123,456

One Hundred Twenty Three Thousand, Four Hundred Fifty Six

Write these numbers correctly in the blanks.

1. 392,599 =

3	9	2	5	9	9
Hundred Thousands	Ten Thousands	Thousands	Hundreds	Tens	Ones

2. 415,675 =

Hundred Thousands	Ten Thousands	Thousands	Hundreds	Tens	Ones

3. 726,211 =

Hundred Thousands	Ten Thousands	Thousands	Hundreds	Tens	Ones

4. 186,452 =

Hundred Thousands	Ten Thousands	Thousands	Hundreds	Tens	Ones

Chapter 2 - Addition

Lesson 1

2-Digit Addition - Regrouping 1

To add multiple digit numbers together, start in the ones place and then use basic addition rules. When the number equals ten or more the first digit carries over to the next spot. This is called **regrouping**.

Step 1: Add the digits in the ones column.	**Step 2**: Carry the 1 over to the top of the tens column.	**Step 3**: Add all the digits in the tens column together.
Hundreds | Tens | Ones	Hundreds | Tens | Ones	Hundreds | Tens | Ones
8 5	1 (carried) / 8 5	1 + 8 + 1 / 8 5
+ 1 7	x 1 7	x 1 7
2	(1) 2	1 0 2

Solve the two-digit addition problems below .

1. 65 + 14 = 79	**2.** 35 + 54	**3.** 11 + 51	**4.** 42 + 35
5. 89 + 10	**6.** 25 + 81	**7.** 47 + 31	**8.** 12 + 26
9. 25 + 44	**10.** 51 + 27	**11.** 19 + 10	**12.** 13 + 34

2-Digit Addition - Regrouping 2

Solve the two-digit addition problems below .

1. 85 + 36	**2.** 24 + 23	**3.** 11 + 78	
4. 46 + 38	**5.** 68 + 45	**6.** 33 + 61	**7.** 17 + 25
8. 95 + 21	**9.** 72 + 14	**10.** 13 + 10	**11.** 21 + 67
12. 37 + 16	**13.** 23 + 68	**14.** 65 + 22	**15.** 88 + 40
16. 20 + 99	**17.** 54 + 32	**18.** 34 + 44	**19.** 70 + 50

2-Digit Addition - Regrouping 3

Solve the two-digit addition problems below .

1. 93 + 73

2. 49 + 85

3. 60 + 78

4. 72 + 59

5. 44 + 11

6. 99 + 66

7. 32 + 12

8. 94 + 57

9. 74 + 39

10. 13 + 74

11. 96 + 24

12. 75 + 50

13. 15 + 69

14. 18 + 87

15. 10 + 15

16 19 + 78

17. 22 + 38

18. 43 + 17

19. 26 + 51

Lesson 2

Symbol Addition 1

Use the symbols to solve the addition problems.

Write out each equation.

□ = 100 ○ = 10 △ = 1

1. □ ○ ○ △ = 121

   100 + 10 + 10 + 1

2. □△△△△△ = ____

   ____

3. □□□□□ ○ = ____

   ____

4. ○○○○△△ = ____

   ____

5. □□○○○○ = ____

   ____

6. □○△△△△ = ____

   ____

7. □□□○△△ = ____

   ____

8. □○○○○△ = ____

   ____

Symbol Addition 2

Use the symbols to solve the addition problems.

Write out each equation.

⏢ = 1000 □ = 100 ○ = 10 △ = 1

1. ⏢ □ ○ △ △ = 1,112
   1000 + 100 + 10 + 1 + 1

2. ⏢⏢⏢□△ = ____
   ____

3. ⏢□□○△△ = ____
   ____

4. ⏢⏢⏢⏢□ = ____
   ____

5. ⏢⏢□□○○ = ____
   ____

6. □○○△△△ = ____
   ____

7. ⏢⏢□○○△ = ____
   ____

8. □□□○○△ = ____
   ____

Lesson 3

Adding 3-Digit Numbers 1

Solve the three-digit addition problems below .

1. 910 + 896	2. 238 + 654	3. 336 + 994	
4. 650 + 273	5. 852 + 470	6. 182 + 649	7. 238 + 151
8. 290 + 764	9. 905 + 675	10. 70 + 134	11. 436 + 528
12. 533 + 343	13. 866 + 498	14. 399 + 249	15. 615 + 99
16. 608 + 422	17. 206 + 840	18. 134 + 428	19. 704 + 271

Adding 3-Digit Numbers 2

Solve the three-digit addition problems below .

1. 701 162 + 910	**2.** 918 867 + 997	**3.** 281 33 + 537	
4. 843 565 + 29	**5.** 224 647 + 777	**6.** 582 412 + 292	**7.** 528 263 + 108
8. 179 343 + 686	**9.** 615 687 + 926	**10.** 135 937 + 439	**11.** 621 415 + 18
12. 682 736 + 529	**13.** 214 568 + 891	**14.** 184 696 + 515	**15.** 125 301 + 296

Adding 3-Digit Numbers 3

Solve the three-digit addition problems below .

1. 781 376 695 + 535	**2.** 123 511 235 + 321	**3.** 600 581 935 + 939	
4. 171 334 863 + 886	**5.** 444 303 224 + 598	**6.** 673 510 576 + 507	**7.** 584 123 11 + 901
8. 256 912 318 + 608	**9.** 319 720 48 + 449	**10.** 793 951 219 + 358	**11.** 273 173 712 + 327
12. 287 358 656 + 180	**13.** 281 42 505 + 210	**14.** 199 439 779 + 416	**15.** 100 156 704 + 222

Lesson 4

Fill in the Blanks

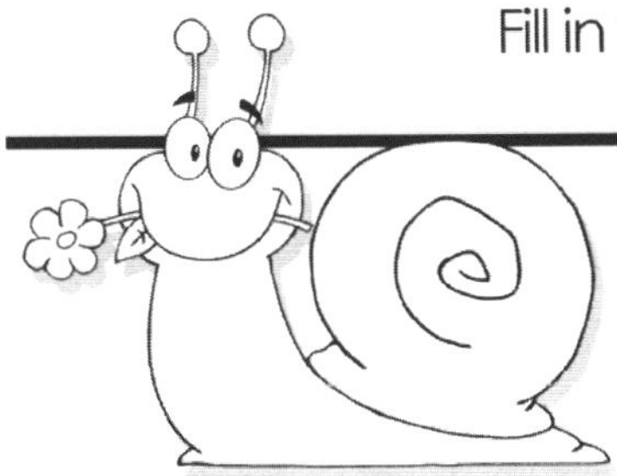

Fill in the blanks to complete each problem.

	1. 1 2 4 + 1 9 1 3 1 5	**2.** 2 __ 9 + __ 3 2 8 7 1
3. 3 4 8 + __ 3 __ 9 7 9	**4.** 6 __ 3 + 2 __ 2 8 4 5	**5.** __ 3 7 + 4 __ 7 5 8 4
6. 5 8 __ + __ 9 1 9 7 4	**7.** 3 7 5 + 1 __ __ 5 8 0	**8.** __ 1 5 + 1 2 __ 2 3 7
9. __ 2 4 + 1 2 3 5 4 7	**10.** 5 __ 4 + __ 6 1 7 8 5	**11.** __ 3 4 + 1 6 __ 3 9 6

Lesson 5

Adding 4-Digit Numbers 1

Solve the four-digit addition problems below.

1. 1,358 + 4,143

5,501

2. 2,429 + 4,632

3. 1,937 + 6,699

4. 6,420 + 1,603

5. 1,620 + 7,091

6. 6,369 + 3,113

7. 3,014 + 1,107

8. 9,908 + 5,287

9. 9,394 + 9,517

10. 3,289 + 3,237

11. 6,922 + 7,801

12. 3,940 + 4,101

13. 3,323 + 4,582

14. 8,129 + 2,035

15. 1,842 + 2,557

Adding 4-Digit Numbers 2

Solve the four-digit addition problems below .

1. 4,914 + 2,553 + 174	**2.** 6,442 + 1,651 + 2,533	**3.** 338 + 2,054 + 8,652
4. 8,681 + 6,602 + 6,389	**5.** 3,362 + 6,187 + 9,746	**6.** 5,759 + 6,973 + 9,969
7. 5,802 + 8,920 + 4,492	**8.** 7,475 + 7,248 + 8,533	**9.** 8,348 + 1,829 + 8,451
10. 6,136 + 3,347 + 1,688	**11.** 2,879 + 1,927 + 4,880	**12.** 8,080 + 7,347 + 6,240

Lesson 6

Addition Squares 1

- Add the numbers going down
- Add the numbers going across
- Then add your answers together, either across or down, to fill in the the last square

3	4	7
2	3	5
5	7	(12)

1.

1	5	
5	2	

2.

2	8	
8	9	

3.

6	3	
3	6	

4.

2	15	
15	2	

5.

25	4	
4	10	

6.

1	8	
8	40	

Addition Squares 2

- Add the numbers going down
- Add the numbers going across
- Then add your answers together, either across or down, to fill in the the last square

3	4	7
2	3	5
5	7	(12)

1.

10	3	
3	10	

2.

5	8	
8	5	

3.

1	7	
7	1	

4.

3	6	
6	12	

5.

70	13	
13	45	

6.

2	36	
36	2	

Chapter 3 - Subtraction

Lesson 1

Subtracting 2-Digit Numbers 1

To subtract and borrow, start with the ones column. If the bottom number is of a greater value, you have to borrow from the next column.

Step 1:
If the bottom number is a greater value than the top number, you need to borrow.

Tens	Ones
8	4
- 1	9

Step 2:
Borrow 10 from the next column. Reducing the 8 to 7 and increasing 4 to 14. Now we are ready to subtract.

Tens	Ones
7	
~~8~~	14
- 1	9
	5

Step 3:
Finish by subtracting the numbers in the tens column.

Tens	Ones
7	
~~8~~	14
- 1	9
6	5

Solve the two-digit subtraction problems below.

1. 23 − 10 = 13

2. 86 − 81

3. 24 − 19

4. 65 − 29

5. 58 − 21

6. 42 − 12

7. 38 − 16

8. 37 − 15

9. 61 − 34

10. 57 − 43

11. 85 − 26

12. 82 − 39

Subtracting 2-Digit Numbers 2

Solve the two-digit subtraction problems below.

1. 85 − 83

2. 94 − 87

3. 50 − 43

4. 38 − 34

5. 66 − 13

6. 77 − 16

7. 36 − 30

8. 99 − 51

9. 79 − 11

10. 54 − 14

11. 29 − 21

12. 74 − 14

13. 47 − 12

14. 69 − 21

15. 68 − 51

16. 85 − 77

17. 98 − 62

18. 79 − 48

19. 59 − 45

Subtracting 2-Digit Numbers 3

Solve the two-digit subtraction problems below .

1. 99 − 55	**2.** 78 − 33	**3.** 68 − 45	
4. 50 − 42	**5.** 48 − 25	**6.** 88 − 33	**7.** 34 − 25
8. 25 − 17	**9.** 77 − 25	**10.** 78 − 37	**11.** 91 − 58
12. 75 − 39	**13.** 54 − 26	**14.** 78 − 17	**15.** 61 − 26
16. 68 − 13	**17.** 11 − 9	**18.** 90 − 72	**19.** 70 − 40

Lesson 2

Subtracting 3-Digit Numbers 1

Solve the three-digit subtraction problems below .

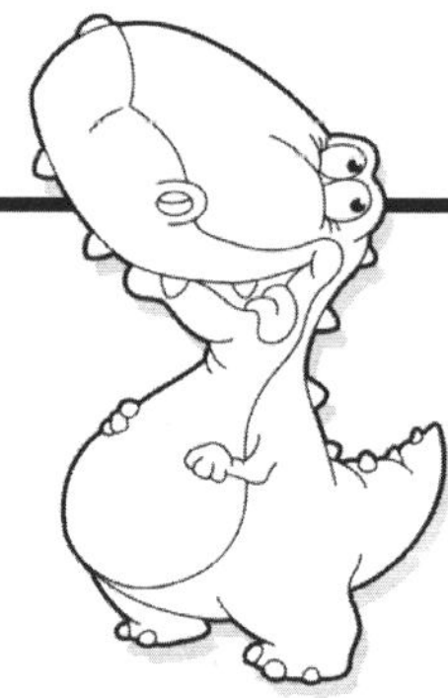

1. 858 − 830

2. 912 − 875

3. 502 − 436

4. 388 − 346

5. 662 − 136

6. 775 − 163

7. 959 − 436

8. 991 − 519

9. 791 − 113

10. 540 − 162

11. 343 − 278

12. 746 − 141

13. 470 − 129

14. 612 − 129

15. 403 − 246

16. 850 − 773

17. 984 − 623

18. 799 − 486

19. 236 − 149

Subtracting 3-Digit Numbers 2

Solve the three-digit subtraction problems below .

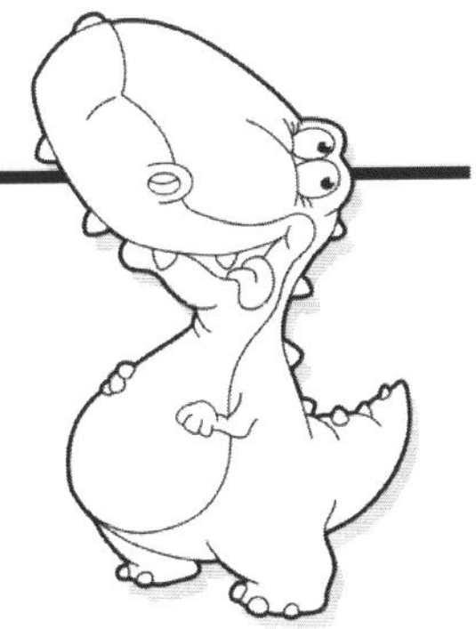

1. 663 − 283

2. 967 − 309

3. 382 − 178

4. 991 − 730

5. 780 − 323

6. 984 − 981

7. 382 − 178

8. 706 − 429

9. 906 − 567

10. 974 − 205

11. 984 − 625

12. 782 − 444

13. 796 − 245

14. 983 − 734

15. 974 − 205

16. 770 − 215

17. 847 − 327

18. 771 − 605

19. 939 − 145

Subtracting 3-Digit Numbers 3

Solve the three-digit subtraction problems below .

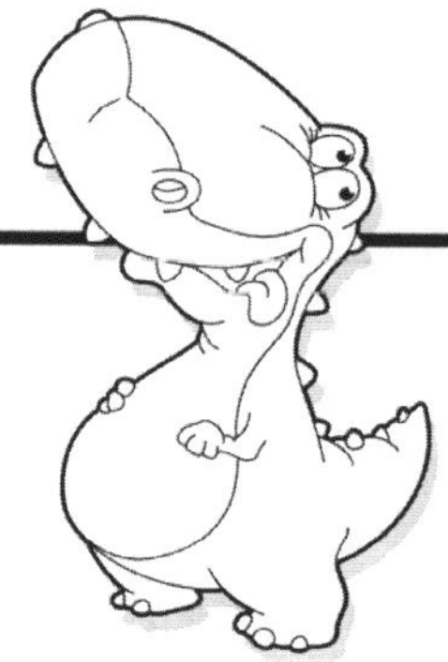

1. $\begin{array}{r} 547 \\ -\ 365 \\ \hline \end{array}$ **2.** $\begin{array}{r} 875 \\ -\ 756 \\ \hline \end{array}$ **3.** $\begin{array}{r} 946 \\ -\ 647 \\ \hline \end{array}$

4. $\begin{array}{r} 321 \\ -\ 215 \\ \hline \end{array}$ **5.** $\begin{array}{r} 697 \\ -\ 610 \\ \hline \end{array}$ **6.** $\begin{array}{r} 257 \\ -\ 101 \\ \hline \end{array}$ **7.** $\begin{array}{r} 473 \\ -\ 318 \\ \hline \end{array}$

8. $\begin{array}{r} 892 \\ -\ 632 \\ \hline \end{array}$ **9.** $\begin{array}{r} 189 \\ -\ 112 \\ \hline \end{array}$ **10.** $\begin{array}{r} 326 \\ -\ 216 \\ \hline \end{array}$ **11.** $\begin{array}{r} 679 \\ -\ 254 \\ \hline \end{array}$

12. $\begin{array}{r} 244 \\ -\ 189 \\ \hline \end{array}$ **13.** $\begin{array}{r} 426 \\ -\ 218 \\ \hline \end{array}$ **14.** $\begin{array}{r} 581 \\ -\ 347 \\ \hline \end{array}$ **15.** $\begin{array}{r} 169 \\ -\ 146 \\ \hline \end{array}$

16. $\begin{array}{r} 671 \\ -\ 435 \\ \hline \end{array}$ **17.** $\begin{array}{r} 731 \\ -\ 229 \\ \hline \end{array}$ **18.** $\begin{array}{r} 843 \\ -\ 251 \\ \hline \end{array}$ **19.** $\begin{array}{r} 222 \\ -\ 118 \\ \hline \end{array}$

Lesson 3

Subtraction Sentences 1

Complete the problems below by filling in the blank with the correct number.

1. ____ - 50 = 35

2. 45 - ____ = 13

3. ____ - 16 = 120

4. 66 - ____ = 24

5. ____ - 14 = 67

6. 109 - ____ = 56

7. ____ - 59 = 24

8. ____ - 31 = 42

9. ____ - 9 = 103

10. ____ - 72 = 2

11. 24 - ____ = 4

12. 89 - ____ = 28

13. 74 - ____ = 37

14. ____ - 56 = 104

15. 101 - ____ = 61

16. 98 - ____ = 41

17. ____ - 65 = 27

18. ____ - 3 = 13

19. ____ - 146 = 210

20. ____ - 0 = 30

Subtraction Sentences 2

Complete the problems below by filling in the blank with the correct number.

1. ____ − 60 = 45

2. 99 − ____ = 19

3. ____ − 50 = 120

4. 47 − ____ = 17

5. ____ − 120 = 15

6. 53 − ____ = 33

7. ____ − 40 = 79

8. ____ − 100 = 99

9. ____ − 0 = 41

10. ____ − 80 = 6

11. 85 − ____ = 35

12. 90 − ____ = 50

13. 108 − ____ = 48

14. ____ − 0 = 15

15. 45 − ____ = 15

16. 187 − ____ = 157

17. ____ − 0 = 187

18. ____ − 40 = 35

19. ____ − 90 = 90

20. ____ − 40 = 121

Lesson 4

Borrow Over Two Zeros

Solve the three-digit subtraction problems below .

1. 400 − 206	**2.** 900 − 309	**3.** 300 − 178	
4. 900 − 107	**5.** 700 − 323	**6.** 981 − 100	**7.** 806 − 219
8. 700 − 386	**9.** 800 − 567	**10.** 400 − 205	**11.** 900 − 281
12. 300 − 86	**13.** 200 − 145	**14.** 800 − 734	**15.** 774 − 396
16. 100 − 54	**17.** 800 − 327	**18.** 700 − 605	**19.** 300 − 234

Lesson 5

Subtracting 4-Digit Numbers 1

Solve the four-digit subtraction problems below .

1. 4,1 3 2 − 2,0 6 1

2. 9,6 6 4 − 7,6 5 5

3. 9,9 9 9 − 1,0 7 9

4. 4,1 2 5 − 1,1 4 5

5. 6,6 9 8 − 3,3 6 7

6. 7,9 5 6 − 3,8 6 5

7. 7,9 3 8 − 2,8 6 7

8. 7,1 5 5 − 2,8 2 1

9. 3,6 4 9 − 8 6 8

10. 5,7 8 8 − 2 2 3

11. 8,3 2 2 − 7 4 9

12. 1 6 6 3 − 5 4 2

13. 5, 8 2 7 − 4, 6 1 4

14. 3, 7 8 5 − 2, 6 3 4

Subtracting 4-Digit Numbers 2

Solve the four-digit subtraction problems below .

1. 5,062 − 1,696

2. 7,776 − 6,872

3. 9,718 − 7,259

4. 1,738 − 1,584

5. 7,417 − 6,556

6. 3,515 − 2,267

7. 9,754 − 5,993

8. 5,621 − 1,995

9. 8,218 − 3,147

10. 2,315 − 390

11. 4,447 − 2,372

12. 5,679 − 5,568

13. 5,154 − 1,700

14. 3,176 − 2,856

Subtracting 4-Digit Numbers 3

Solve the four-digit subtraction problems below .

1. 3,808 − 1,919

2. 4,445 − 178

3. 3,608 − 2,564

4. 2,878 − 289

5. 9,376 − 5,697

6. 4,206 − 4,187

7. 2,525 − 1,636

8. 4,136 − 3,647

9. 1,691 − 516

10. 7,248 − 4,559

11. 2,028 − 798

12. 9,136 − 2,641

13. 4,844 − 1,491

14. 4,952 − 968

Subtracting 4-Digit Numbers 4

Solve the four-digit subtraction problems below .

1. 5,791 − 1,101
2. 6,434 − 590
3. 5,079 − 3,034
4. 4,834 − 2,263
5. 3,897 − 2,113
6. 6,313 − 2,091
7. 9,776 − 4,370
8. 9,190 − 3,293
9. 8,957 − 2,835
10. 9,752 − 4,743
11. 7,499 − 2,170
12. 3,146 − 2,738
13. 9,181 − 145
14. 5,914 − 5,238

Chapter 4 - Division

Division

- Division is a way to find out how many times one number is counted in another number.
- The $\div$ sign means " divided by".
- Another way to divide is to use $\overline{)}$.
- The dividend is the larger number that is divided by the smaller number, the divisor.
- The answer of a division problem is called the quotient.

$\div$ means divide

$6 \div 2 = 3$

dividend **divisor** **quotient**

- $6 \div 2 = 3$ is read "6 divided by 2 is equal to 3".
- In $6 \div 2 = 3$, the divisor is 2, the dividend is 6 and the quotient is 3.

$\overline{)}$ means divide

$2\overline{)10}$ with quotient 5

divisor **dividend** **quotient**

- $\begin{array}{r}5\\2\overline{)10}\end{array}$ is read "10 divided by 2 is equal to 5".
- In $\begin{array}{r}5\\2\overline{)10}\end{array}$, the divisor is 2, the dividend is 10 and the quotient is 5.

Lesson 1

Dividing Objects 1

Divide the objects equally by the animals for each group.

Objects	Animals	Answer
10 Bananas		5
15 Nuts		
9 Cheeses		
14 Bones		
20 Carrots		

Dividing Objects 2

Divide each group by the numbers in each box and write the answers.

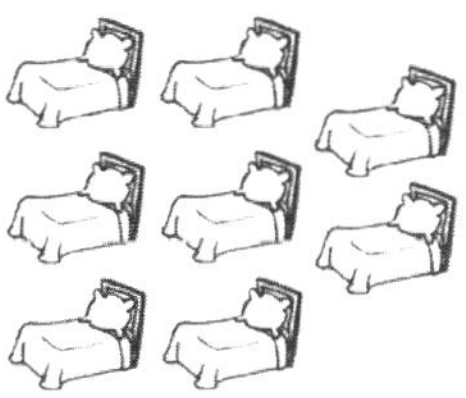

÷ 4 = 2

÷ 2 = 4

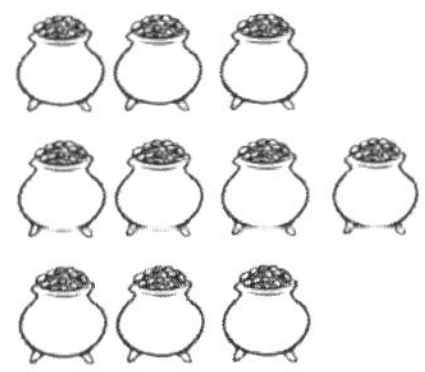

÷ 5 = ___

÷ 2 = ___

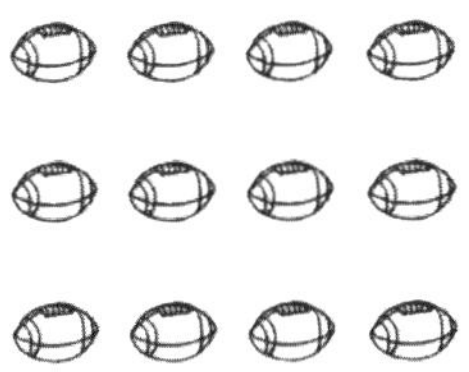

÷ 3 = ___

÷ 2 = ___

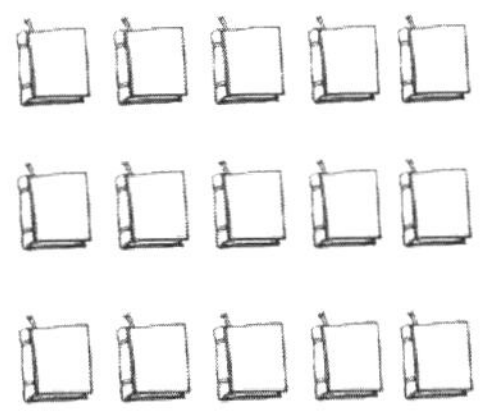

÷ 3 = ___

÷ 5 = ___

÷ 5 = ___

÷ 4 =

÷ 2 = ___

÷ 8 = ___

÷ 4 = ___

÷ 2 = ___

Lesson 2

Division Wording and Terms

Complete each sentence.

1. $\begin{array}{r} 2 \\ 9\overline{)18} \end{array}$ is read " 18 divided by 9 is equal to 2."
2. $\begin{array}{r} 4 \\ 4\overline{)16} \end{array}$ is read " ___ divided by ___ is equal to ___."
3. $\begin{array}{r} 25 \\ 5\overline{)125} \end{array}$ is read " ___ divided by ___ is equal to ___."
4. $15 \div 3 = 5$ is read " ___ divided by ___ is equal to ___."
5. $100 \div 10 = 10$ is read " ___ divided by ___ is equal to ___."
6. $72 \div 9 = 8$ is read " ___ divided by ___ is equal to ___."
7. $\begin{array}{r} 3 \\ 4\overline{)12} \end{array}$ The divisor is ____, the dividend is ____, the quotient is ____."
8. $\begin{array}{r} 6 \\ 5\overline{)30} \end{array}$ The divisor is ____, the dividend is ____, the quotient is ____."
9. $\begin{array}{r} 7 \\ 6\overline{)42} \end{array}$ The divisor is ____, the dividend is ____, the quotient is ____."
10. $\begin{array}{r} 8 \\ 8\overline{)64} \end{array}$ The divisor is ____, the dividend is ____, the quotient is ____."
11. $\begin{array}{r} 5 \\ 2\overline{)10} \end{array}$ The divisor is ____, the dividend is ____, the quotient is ____."
12. $\begin{array}{r} 7 \\ 3\overline{)21} \end{array}$ The divisor is ____, the dividend is ____, the quotient is ____."

Lesson 3

Dividing by 10 and 100

Use division to answer the following questions.

1. 70 ÷ 10 = 7
2. 700 ÷ 100 = ___
3. 4600 ÷ 100 = ___
4. 5200 ÷ 100 = ___
5. 280 ÷ 10 = ___
6. 370 ÷ 10 = ___
7. 2700 ÷ 100 = ___
8. 330 ÷ 10 = ___
9. 220 ÷ 10 = ___
10. 990 ÷ 10 = ___
11. 5900 ÷ 100 = ___
12. 820 ÷ 10 = ___
13. 800 ÷ 10 = ___
14. 900 ÷ 10 = ___
15. 3000 ÷ 100 = ___
16. 970 ÷ 10 = ___
17. 460 ÷ 10 = ___
18. 950 ÷ 10 = ___
19. 590 ÷ 10 = ___
20. 650 ÷ 10 = ___

Lesson 4

Writing Division

Write out each problem and then solve it.

1. John has 24 toy planes. He wants to divide them into equal groups.
Show two ways he can write that.

$24 \div 8 = 3$ $24 \div 6 = 4$

2. Mary has 15 strawberries. She wants to divide them into equal groups.
Show two ways she can write that.

________________ ________________

3. Jane has 10 colors. She wants to divide them into equal groups.
Show two ways she can write that.

________________ ________________

4. Eric has 50 cards. He wants to divide them into equal groups.
Show two ways he can write that.

________________ ________________

Lesson 5

Basic Division 1

Solve each problem.

1. $\begin{array}{r} 6 \\ 9\overline{)54} \end{array}$

2. $4\overline{)20}$

3. $4\overline{)24}$

4. $3\overline{)12}$

5. $8\overline{)32}$

6. $9\overline{)81}$

7. $2\overline{)16}$

8. $7\overline{)63}$

9. $3\overline{)24}$

10. $7\overline{)56}$

Basic Division 2

Solve each problem.

1. $\begin{array}{r} 10 \\ 10\overline{)100} \end{array}$

2. $6\overline{)24}$

3. $5\overline{)25}$

4. $9\overline{)45}$

5. $6\overline{)42}$

6. $25\overline{)25}$

7. $25\overline{)125}$

8. $11\overline{)110}$

9. $7\overline{)21}$

10. $6\overline{)36}$

Lesson 6

Divide by 2 Both Ways

Use division to answer the following questions.

1. $40 \div 2 =$ 20
2. $8 \div 2 =$ ___
3. $50 \div 2 =$ ___
4. $30 \div 2 =$ ___
5. $12 \div 2 =$ ___
6. $20 \div 2 =$ ___
7. $10 \div 2 =$ ___
8. $50 \div 2 =$ ___
9. $38 \div 2 =$ ___
10. $24 \div 2 =$ ___

11. $2\overline{)44}$
12. $2\overline{)60}$
13. $2\overline{)20}$
14. $2\overline{)84}$
15. $2\overline{)12}$
16. $2\overline{)36}$

Lesson 7

Divide by 5 Both Ways

Use division to answer the following questions.

1. $40 \div 5 =$ 8
2. $90 \div 5 =$ ___
3. $50 \div 5 =$ ___
4. $30 \div 5 =$ ___
5. $15 \div 5 =$ ___
6. $20 \div 5 =$ ___
7. $10 \div 5 =$ ___
8. $50 \div 5 =$ ___
9. $35 \div 5 =$ ___
10. $25 \div 5 =$ ___

---

11. $5\overline{)85}$
12. $5\overline{)30}$
13. $5\overline{)65}$
14. $5\overline{)90}$
15. $5\overline{)105}$
16. $5\overline{)200}$

Lesson 8

Division Fill in the Blanks 1

Complete the following division problems by filling in the correct missing numbers.

1. 14 ÷ 2 = 7
2. 15 ÷ ___ = 3
3. ___ ÷ 7 = 1
4. ___ ÷ 5 = 2
5. 49 ÷ ___ = 7
6. 54 ÷ ___ = 6
7. ___ ÷ 6 = 3
8. 20 ÷ ___ = 2
9. 25 ÷ ___ = 5
10. 16 ÷ ___ = 4
11. ___ ÷ 6 = 6
12. 12 ÷ ___ = 2
13. 90 ÷ ___ = 9
14. ___ ÷ 9 = 4
15. 45 ÷ ___ = 9
16. 56 ÷ ___ = 8
17. ___ ÷ 10 = 10
18. 40 ÷ ___ = 4
19. ___ ÷ 4 = 10
20. ___ ÷ 5 = 3

Division Fill in the Blanks 2

Complete the following division problems by filling in the correct missing numbers.

1. 30 ÷ 5 = 6
2. 45 ÷ ___ = 9
3. ___ ÷ 9 = 7
4. ___ ÷ 1 = 29
5. 18 ÷ ___ = 9
6. 21 ÷ ___ = 3
7. ___ ÷ 6 = 8
8. 10 ÷ ___ = 2
9. 28 ÷ ___ = 7
10. 12 ÷ ___ = 4
11. ___ ÷ 4 = 23
12. 36 ÷ ___ = 4
13. 80 ÷ ___ = 8
14. ___ ÷ 11 = 5
15. 42 ÷ ___ = 7
16. 32 ÷ ___ = 4
17. ___ ÷ 2 = 11
18. 35 ÷ ___ = 5
19. ___ ÷ 7 = 2
20. ___ ÷ 4 = 4

Chapter 5 - Fractions

Fractions

Fractions are the numbers that make up part of a whole.

Lesson 1

Identifying Fractions

Color $\frac{1}{2}$ of each shape.

1. 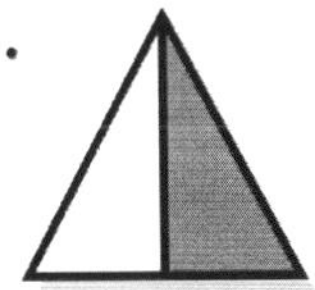

2. 

3. 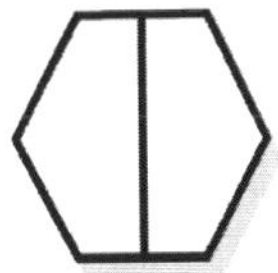

Color $\frac{1}{3}$ of each shape.

4. 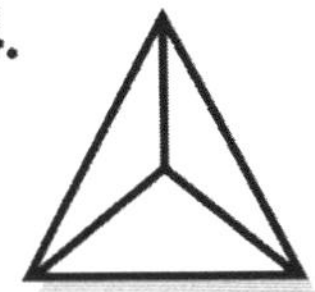

5. 

6. 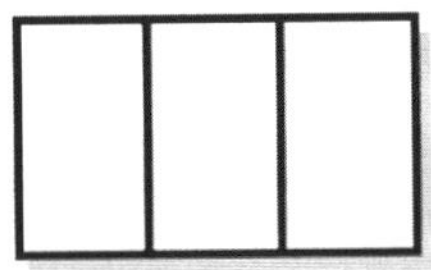

Color $\frac{1}{4}$ of each shape.

7. 

8. 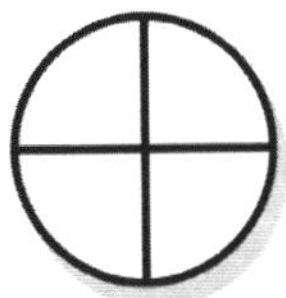

9. 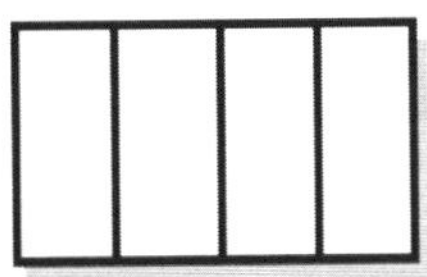

Lesson 2

Explaining Fractions 1

A fraction names a part of a whole. It can also be used to name a part of a group or set.

Fractions are made up of two parts: the **numerator** and the **denominator**.

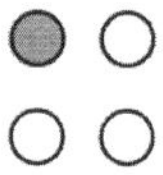 → $\frac{1}{4}$

1 ← The numerator is the number of shaded objects.

4 ← The denominator is the total number of objects.

Write what fraction of each set is shaded in.

1. 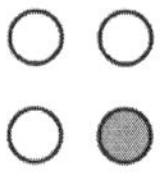 = $\frac{1}{4}$

2. 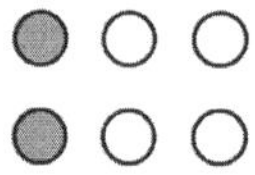 = ☐

3. 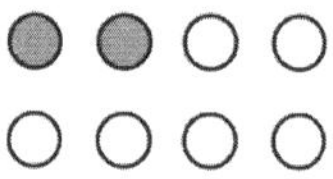 = ☐

4. 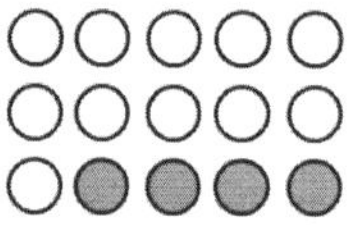 = ☐

5. 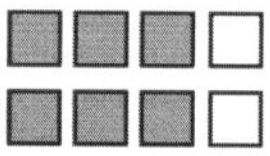 = ☐

6. 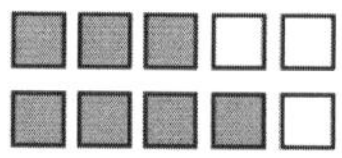 = ☐

7. 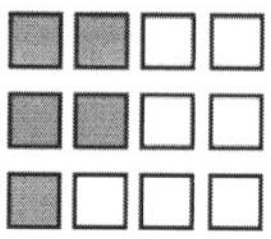 = ☐

8. 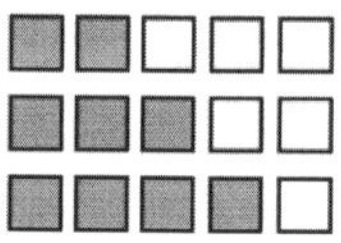 = ☐

Explaining Fractions 2

A fraction names a part of a whole. It can also be used to name a part of a group or set.

Fractions are made up of two parts: the **numerator** and the **denominator**.

● ○
○ ○ → $\frac{1}{4}$

1 ← The numerator is the number of shaded objects.

4 ← The denominator is the total number of objects.

Color each set to match the fraction.

1. $\frac{1}{4}$ = ○ ○ / ○ ●

2. $\frac{2}{8}$ = ○ ○ ○ / ○ ○ ○

3. $\frac{1}{8}$ = ○ ○ ○ ○ / ○ ○ ○ ○

4. $\frac{7}{15}$ = ○○○○○ / ○○○○○ / ○○○○○

5. $\frac{3}{8}$ = □□□□ / □□□□

6. $\frac{6}{10}$ = □□□□□ / □□□□□

7. $\frac{1}{2}$ = □□□□ / □□□□ / □□□□

8. $\frac{5}{15}$ = □□□□□ / □□□□□ / □□□□□

Lesson 3

Matching Fractions

Draw a line to match the fractions.

$\frac{1}{3}$

$\frac{1}{4}$

$\frac{2}{3}$

$\frac{3}{8}$

$\frac{1}{2}$

Lesson 4

Writing Fractions 1

Write the fraction shown in each shape.
Write the shaded amount as the top number.

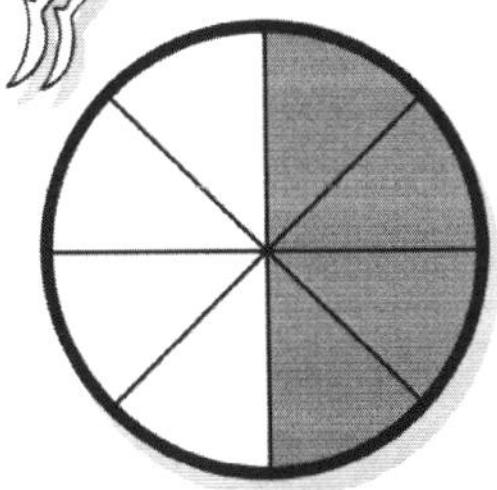 $= \frac{4}{8}$

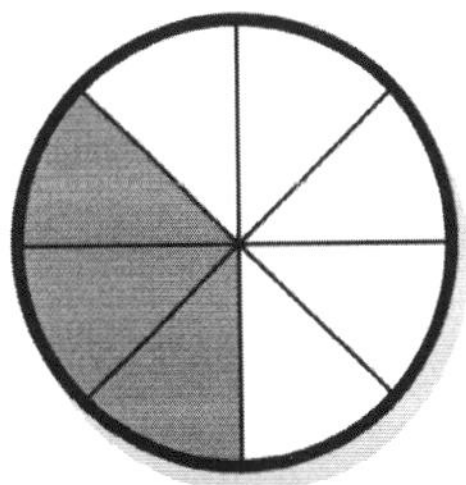 = ___

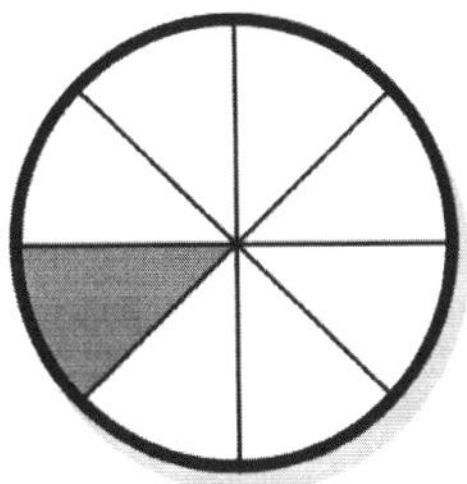 = ___

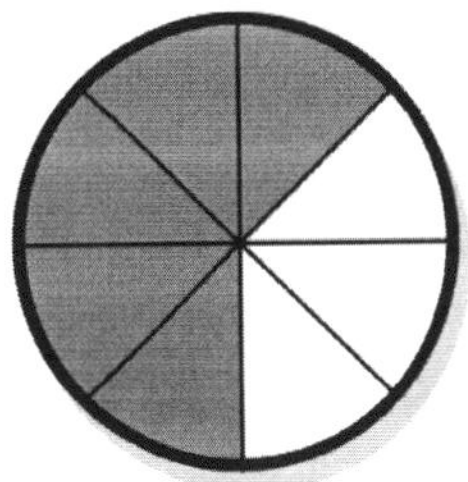 = ___

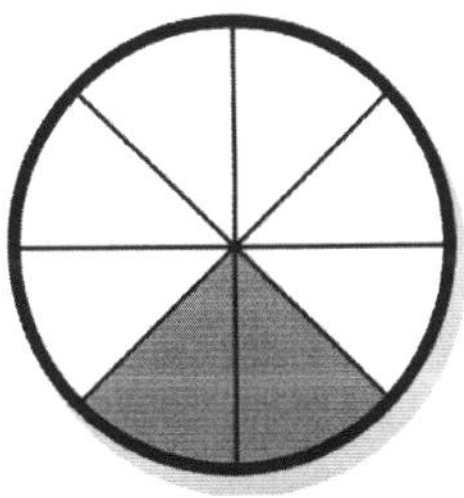 = ___

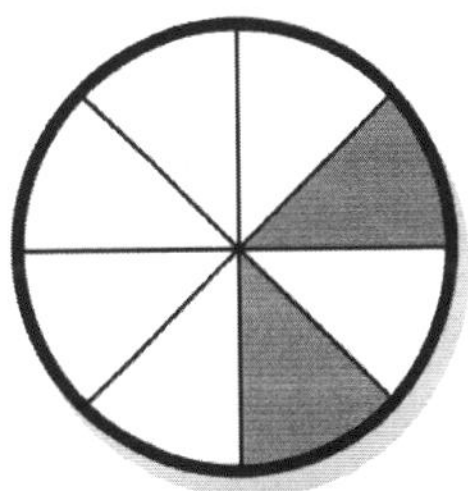 = ___

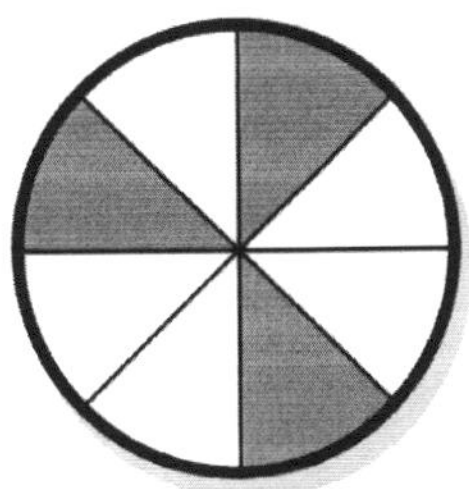 = ___

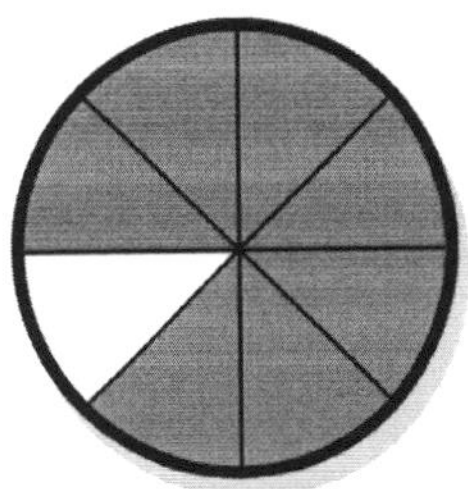 = ___

Writing Fractions 2

Write the fraction shown in each shape.
Write the shaded amount as the top number.

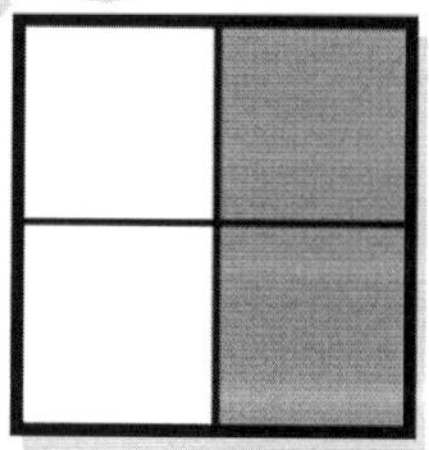 = $\frac{2}{4}$

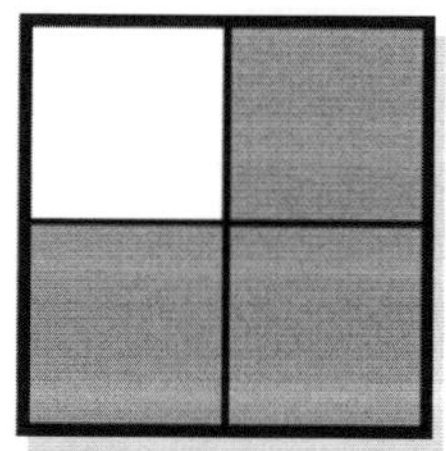 = ___

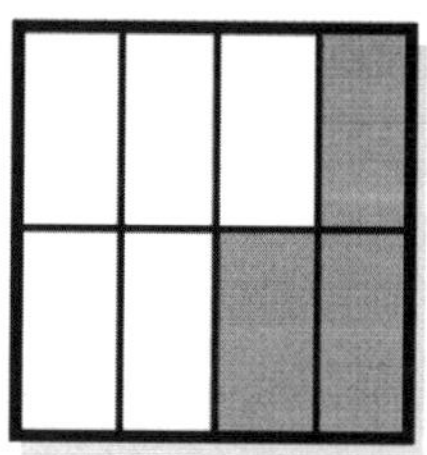 = ___

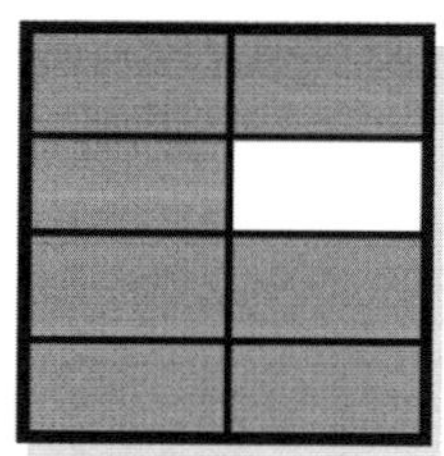 = ___

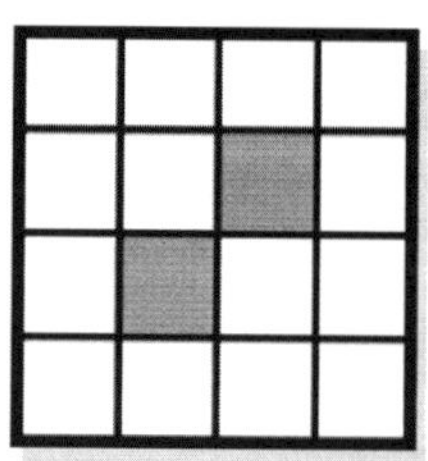 = ___

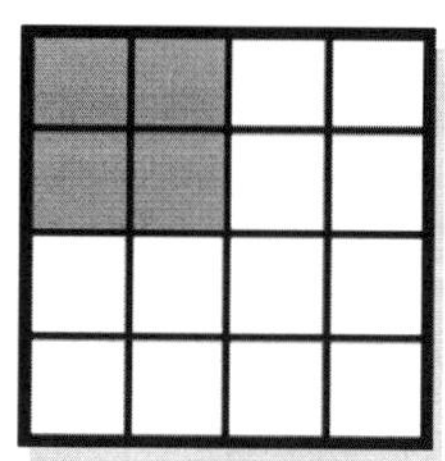 = ___

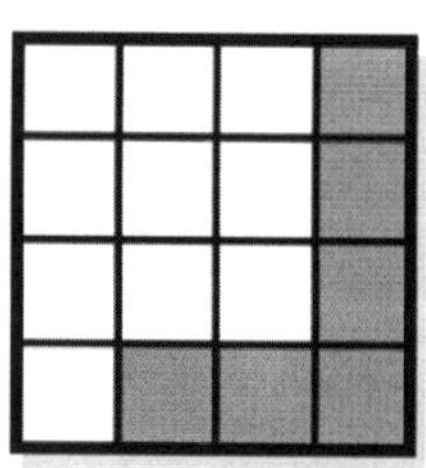 = ___

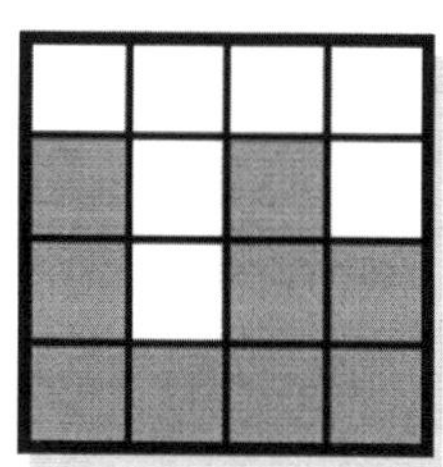 = ___

Lesson 5

Making Fractions

Color each shape to match the fraction.

$\frac{1}{4}$ = 

$\frac{1}{2}$ = 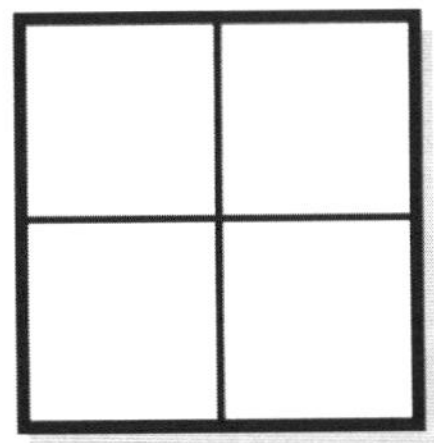

$\frac{3}{8}$ = 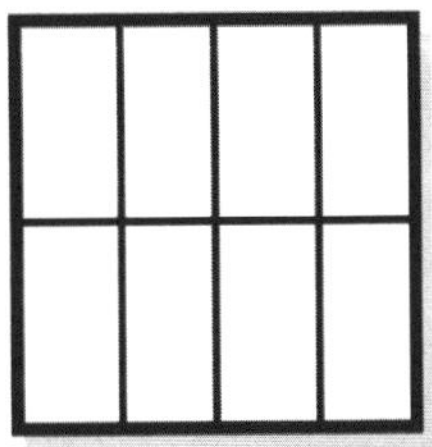

$\frac{5}{8}$ = 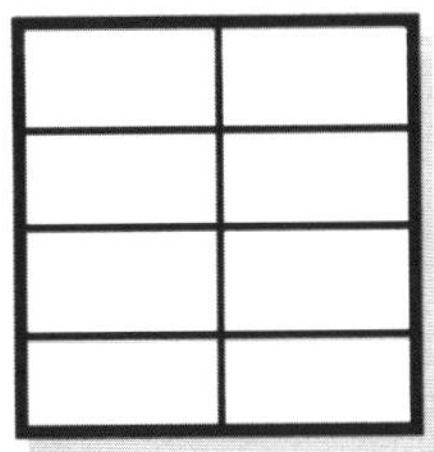

$\frac{5}{16}$ = 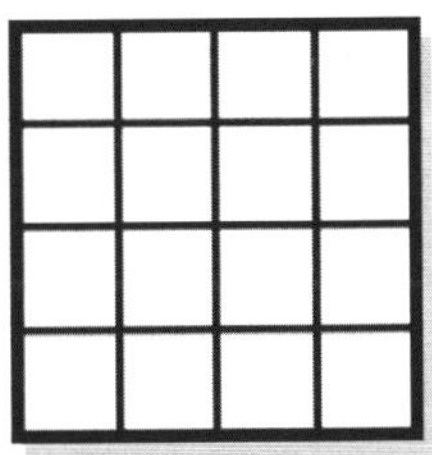

$\frac{9}{16}$ = 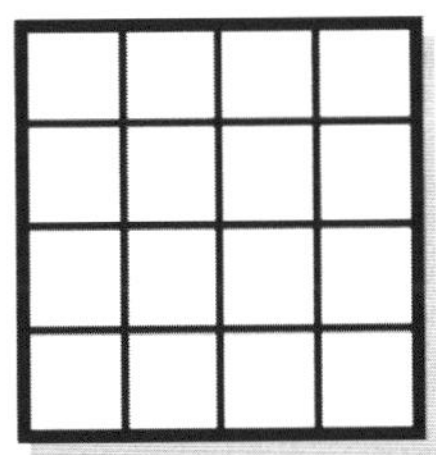

$\frac{2}{16}$ = 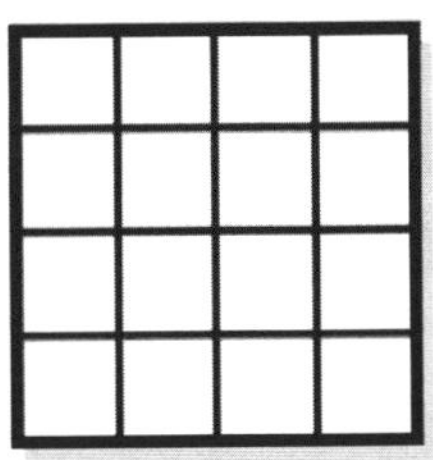

$\frac{7}{16}$ = 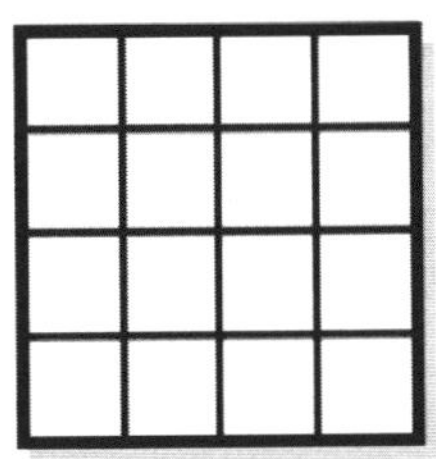

Lesson 6

Whole Numbers and Fractions

The whole number **1** can be shown by many fractions.
When the numerator and denominator match, the fraction equals **1**.

$\frac{6}{6} = 1$	$\frac{8}{8} = 1$	$\frac{3}{3} = 1$

Any whole number can be shown as a fraction iby using **1** for the denominator.

$2 = \frac{2}{1}$	$4 = \frac{4}{1}$	$9 = \frac{9}{1}$

Complete the fractions.

1. $1 = \frac{5}{5}$ **2.** $1 = \frac{\_\_}{8}$ **3.** $1 = \frac{3}{\_\_}$

4. $1 = \frac{\_\_}{14}$ **5.** $1 = \frac{6}{\_\_}$ **6.** $1 = \frac{\_\_}{10}$

Write the fraction that equals the whole number.

1. $5 = \frac{5}{1}$ **2.** $14 =$ _____ **3.** $9 =$ _____

4. $72 =$ _____ **5.** $3 =$ _____ **6.** $18 =$ _____

Lesson 7

Identifying Fractions

Color the correct number of objects for each fraction.

1. $\frac{5}{6}$ 

2. $\frac{1}{3}$ 

3. $\frac{7}{10}$ 

4. $\frac{1}{2}$ 

5. $\frac{1}{3}$ 

6. $\frac{3}{10}$ 

7. $\frac{1}{4}$ 

8. $\frac{2}{3}$ 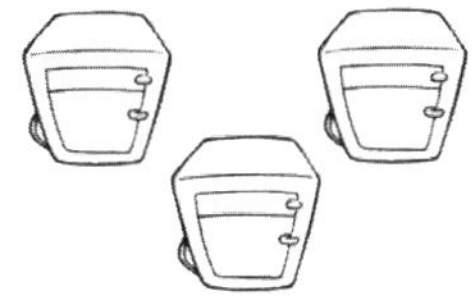

Lesson 8

Comparing Fractions

Just because two fractions are the same, that does not mean they are the same amount.

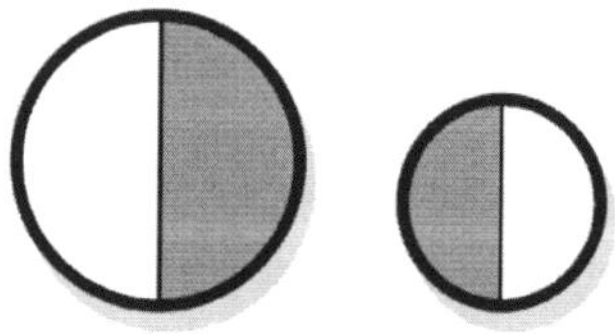

A B

Half of each circle is shaded.
Notice that shape **A** is larger than **B**.
They each show a different amount.

Here are two different ways to write this:

$\frac{1}{2}$ of **A** is greater than $\frac{1}{2}$ of **B** **OR** $\frac{1}{2}$ **A** $\boxed{>}$ $\frac{1}{2}$ **B**

Write out the fractions, then compare the fractions.

1.

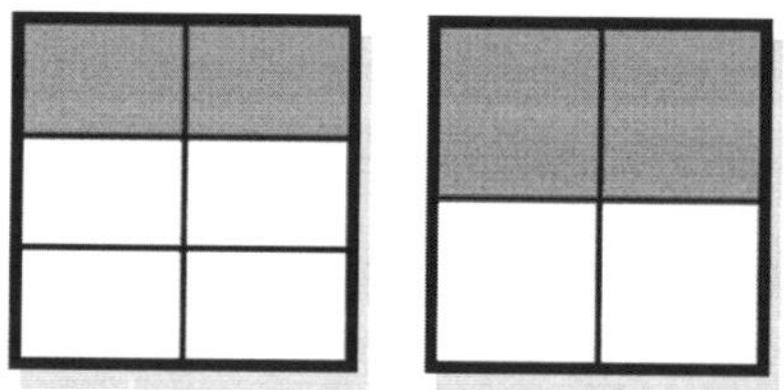

$\frac{2}{6}$ $\boxed{<}$ $\frac{2}{4}$

2.

— □ —

2.

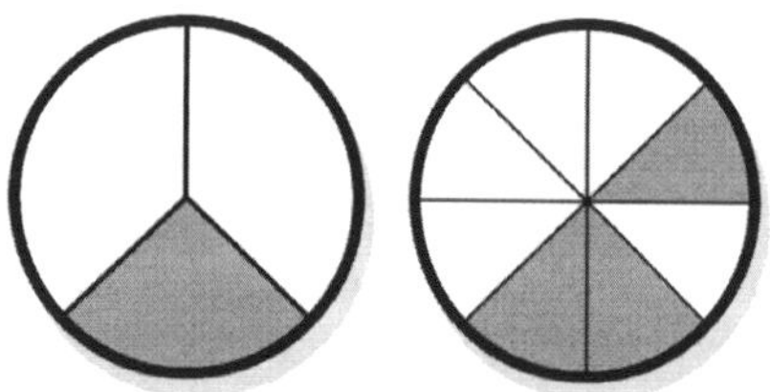

— □ —

2.

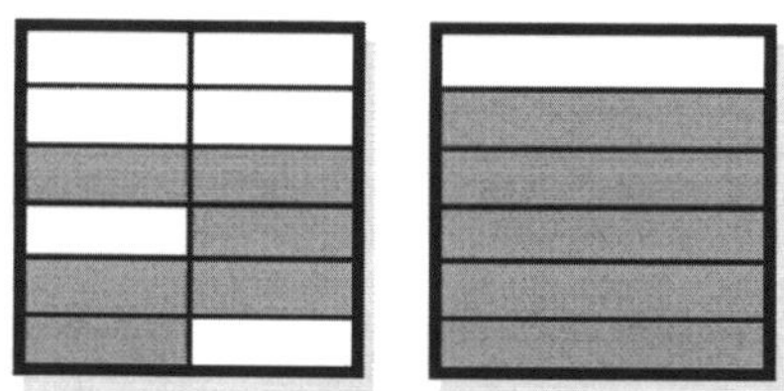

— □ —

Lesson 9

Choosing Fractions

Compare the fractions. Answer if each set is less than, greater than or equal.

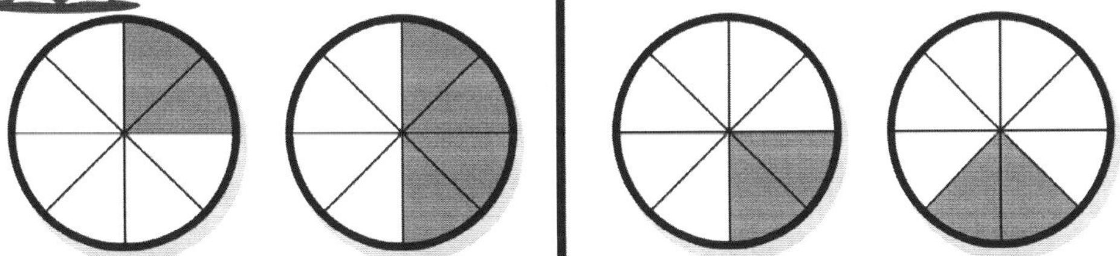

$\frac{2}{8}$ < $\frac{4}{8}$ | $\frac{1}{4}$ □ $\frac{2}{8}$

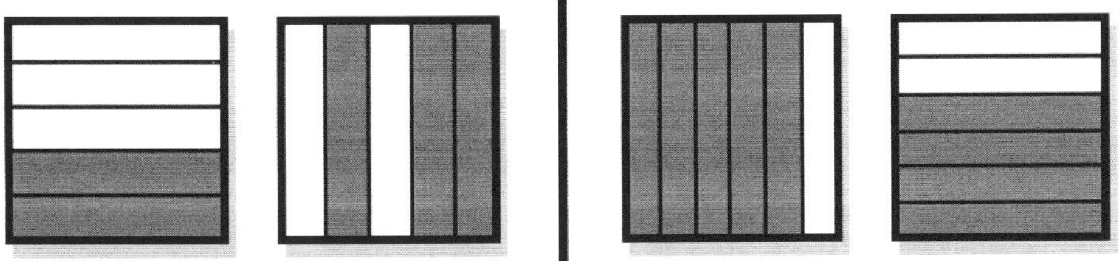

$\frac{2}{5}$ □ $\frac{3}{5}$ | $\frac{5}{6}$ □ $\frac{2}{3}$

$\frac{1}{4}$ □ $\frac{1}{2}$ | $\frac{2}{5}$ □ $\frac{1}{5}$

Lesson 10

Fractions and Values

Circle the fraction that matches the shaded parts in each shape.

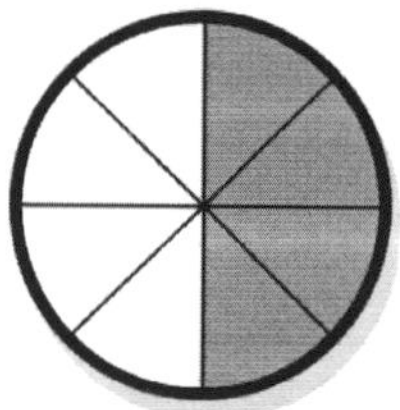

$\frac{3}{4}$ $\frac{1}{2}$ $\frac{1}{8}$

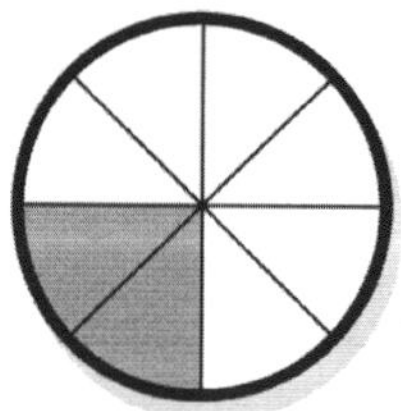

$\frac{1}{2}$ $\frac{1}{8}$ $\frac{1}{4}$

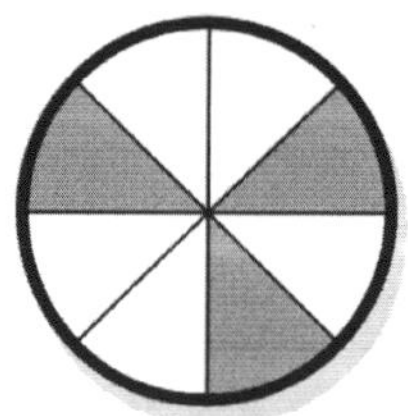

$\frac{3}{8}$ $\frac{1}{2}$ $\frac{2}{4}$

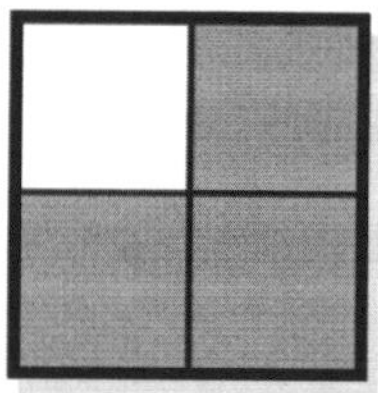

$\frac{3}{4}$ $\frac{1}{2}$ $\frac{1}{8}$

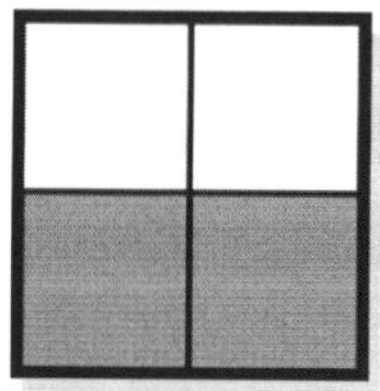

$\frac{1}{2}$ $\frac{3}{4}$ $\frac{1}{4}$

$\frac{2}{3}$ $\frac{1}{2}$ $\frac{1}{4}$

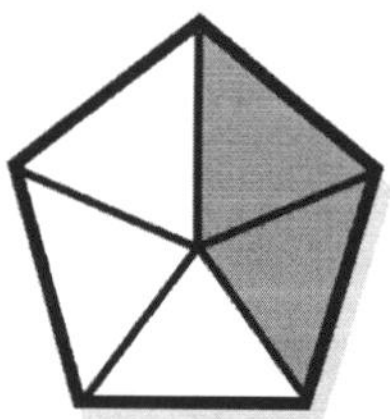

$\frac{3}{4}$ $\frac{2}{5}$ $\frac{1}{8}$

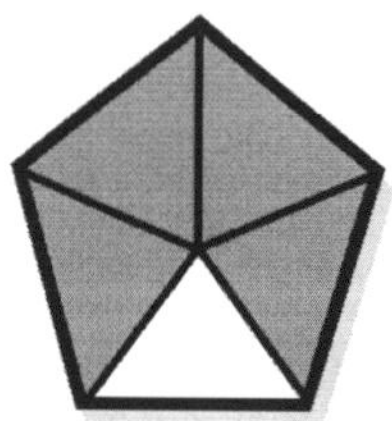

$\frac{4}{5}$ $\frac{1}{4}$ $\frac{3}{5}$

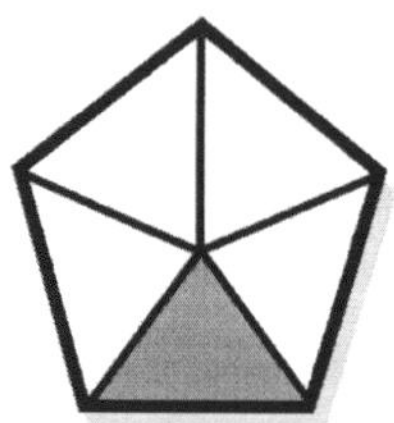

$\frac{3}{5}$ $\frac{1}{3}$ $\frac{1}{5}$

Chapter 6 - Multiplication

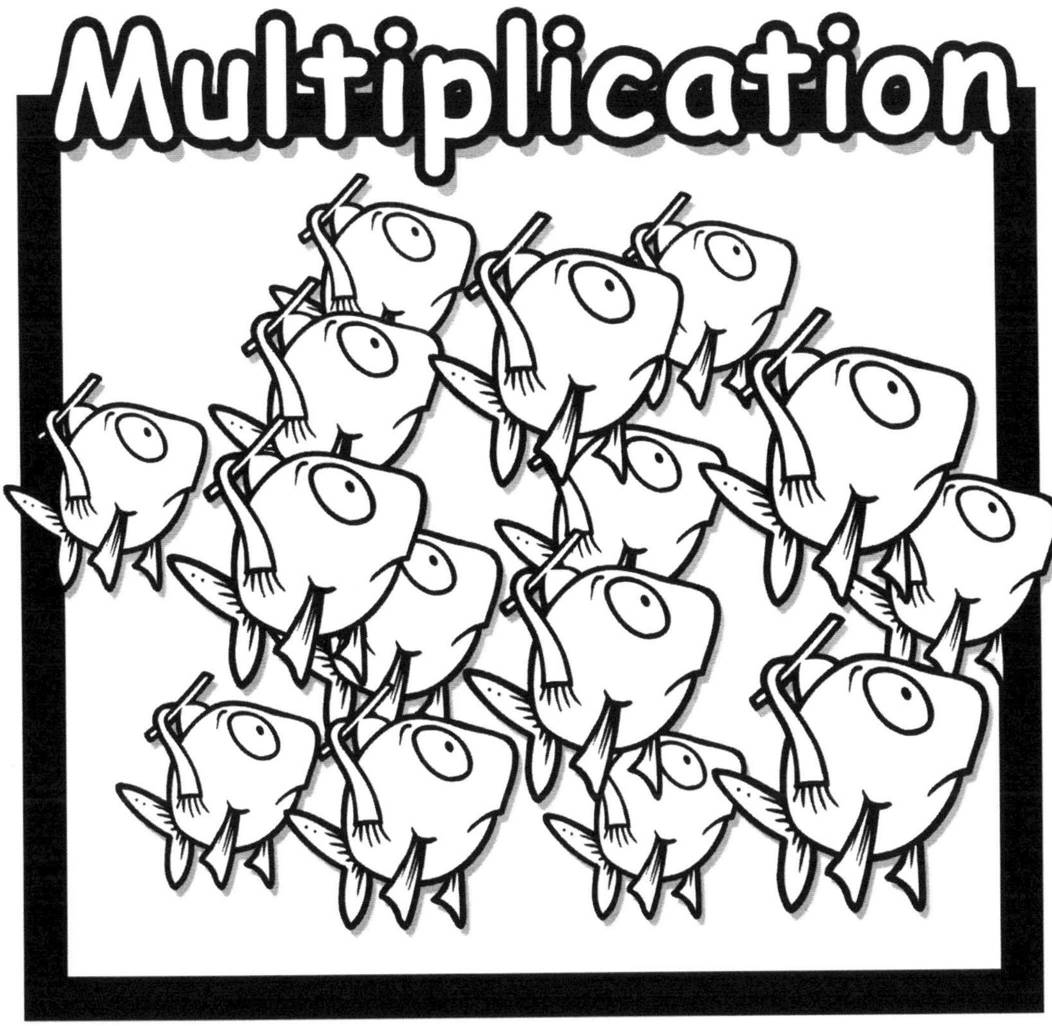

Lesson 1

Multiplication Rules

Multiplication is the way we find the sum of the same number a certain amount of times.

$4 \times 2 = 8$

$2 + 2 + 2 + 2 = 8$

□□ □□ □□ □□

$2 \times 5 = 10$

$5 + 5 = 10$

□□ □□
□□ □□
□ □

Break each group down by writing them out, then adding them together.

1. $3 \times 2 = 6$

___ + ___ + ___ = ___

2. $3 \times 4 = 12$

___ + ___ + ___ = ___

3. $4 \times 4 = 16$

___ + ___ + ___ + ___ = ___

4. $4 \times 5 = 20$

___ + ___ + ___ + ___ = ___

5. $3 \times 8 = 24$

___ + ___ + ___ = ___

6. $4 \times 10 = 40$

___ + ___ + ___ + ___ = ___

7. $2 \times 6 = 12$

___ + ___ = ___

8. $3 \times 6 = 18$

___ + ___ + ___ = ___

Lesson 2

Multiplication by 1

The answer to a multiplication problem is called the **product**.

Switching the order doesn't matter. The product will always be the same.

1	1	1	1	1	1	1	1	1	1
x 0	x 1	x 2	x 3	x 4	x 5	x 6	x 7	x 8	x 9
0	1	2	3	4	5	6	7	8	9

0	1	2	3	4	5	6	7	8	9
x 1	x 1	x 1	x 1	x 1	x 1	x 1	x 1	x 1	x 1
0	1	2	3	4	5	6	7	8	9

Find the product.

1.	**2.**	**3.**	**4.**	**5.**	**6.**	**7.**
2	4	1	9	1	6	2
x 0	x 1	x 1	x 1	x 9	x 1	x 1
0						

8.	**9.**	**10.**	**11.**	**12.**	**13.**	**14.**
8	1	0	3	1	1	5
x 1	x 6	x 9	x 1	x 4	x 6	x 1

15.	**16.**	**17.**	**18.**	**19.**	**20.**	**21.**
3	4	1	7	1	1	0
x 1	x 0	x 2	x 1	x 8	x 7	x 1

Lesson 3

Multiplication by 2

The answer to a multiplication problem is called the **product**.

Switching the order doesn't matter. The product will always be the same.

2 x 0 0	2 x 1 2	2 x 2 4	2 x 3 6	2 x 4 8	2 x 5 10	2 x 6 12	2 x 7 14	2 x 8 16	2 x 9 18

0 x 2 0	1 x 2 2	2 x 2 4	3 x 2 6	4 x 2 8	5 x 2 10	6 x 2 12	7 x 2 14	8 x 2 16	9 x 2 18

Find the product.

1. 9 x 2 18	**2.** 2 x 4	**3.** 8 x 2	**4.** 1 x 7	**5.** 2 x 9	**6.** 2 x 5	**7.** 7 x 1
8. 2 x 2	**9.** 3 x 2	**10.** 2 x 3	**11.** 9 x 2	**12.** 8 x 1	**13.** 2 x 7	**14.** 5 x 2
15. 0 x 2	**16.** 2 x 6	**17.** 8 x 2	**18.** 5 x 0	**19.** 4 x 1	**20.** 2 x 1	**21.** 8 x 1

Lesson 4

Multiplication by 3

The answer to a multiplication problem is called the **product**.

Switching the order doesn't matter. The product will always be the same.

3	3	3	3	3	3	3	3	3	3
x 0	x 1	x 2	x 3	x 4	x 5	x 6	x 7	x 8	x 9
0	3	6	9	12	15	18	21	24	27

0	1	2	3	4	5	6	7	8	9
x 3	x 3	x 3	x 3	x 3	x 3	x 3	x 3	x 3	x 3
0	3	6	9	12	15	18	21	24	27

Find the product.

1. 3	**2.** 9	**3.** 2	**4.** 2	**5.** 3	**6.** 4	**7.** 9
x 2	x 0	x 2	x 7	x 8	x 3	x 2
6						

8. 3	**9.** 7	**10.** 2	**11.** 9	**12.** 7	**13.** 5	**14.** 3
x 8	x 0	x 8	x 3	x 3	x 0	x 3

15. 2	**16.** 7	**17.** 0	**18.** 5	**19.** 1	**20.** 3	**21.** 6
x 1	x 1	x 0	x 3	x 9	x 5	x 3

Lesson 5

Multiplication by 4

The answer to a multiplication problem is called the **product**.

Switching the order doesn't matter. The product will always be the same.

4 x 0 = 0	4 x 1 = 4	4 x 2 = 8	4 x 3 = 12	4 x 4 = 16	4 x 5 = 20	4 x 6 = 24	4 x 7 = 28	4 x 8 = 32	4 x 9 = 36
0 x 4 = 0	1 x 4 = 4	2 x 4 = 8	3 x 4 = 12	4 x 4 = 16	5 x 4 = 20	6 x 4 = 24	7 x 4 = 28	8 x 4 = 32	9 x 4 = 36

Find the product.

1. 3 x 1 = 3
2. 4 x 0
3. 4 x 5
4. 3 x 4
5. 1 x 4
6. 2 x 8
7. 0 x 3

8. 7 x 4
9. 2 x 4
10. 1 x 2
11. 4 x 9
12. 4 x 5
13. 8 x 4
14. 4 x 1

15. 0 x 1
16. 6 x 4
17. 2 x 9
18. 3 x 9
19. 4 x 3
20. 6 x 2
21. 9 x 3

Lesson 6

Multiplication by 5

The answer to a multiplication problem is called the **product**.

Switching the order doesn't matter. The product will always be the same.

5	5	5	5	5	5	5	5	5	5
x 0	x 1	x 2	x 3	x 4	x 5	x 6	x 7	x 8	x 9
0	5	10	15	20	25	30	35	40	45

0	1	2	3	4	5	6	7	8	9
x 5	x 5	x 5	x 5	x 5	x 5	x 5	x 5	x 5	x 5
0	5	10	15	20	25	30	35	40	45

Find the product.

1. 4 x 3 = 12

2. 5 x 2

3. 7 x 5

4. 3 x 6

5. 0 x 5

6. 5 x 1

7. 6 x 3

8. 8 x 5

9. 7 x 0

10. 2 x 8

11. 6 x 5

12. 5 x 5

13. 1 x 4

14. 9 x 5

15. 2 x 9

16. 8 x 2

17. 0 x 4

18. 5 x 3

19. 1 x 9

20. 5 x 2

21. 6 x 3

Lesson 7

Multiplication by 6

The answer to a multiplication problem is called the **product**.

Switching the order doesn't matter. The product will always be the same.

6	6	6	6	6	6	6	6	6	6
x 0	x 1	x 2	x 3	x 4	x 5	x 6	x 7	x 8	x 9
0	6	12	18	24	30	36	42	48	54

0	1	2	3	4	5	6	7	8	9
x 6	x 6	x 6	x 6	x 6	x 6	x 6	x 6	x 6	x 6
0	6	12	18	24	30	36	42	48	54

Find the product.

1. 0 x 6 = 0

2. 9 x 6

3. 5 x 3

4. 4 x 2

5. 6 x 2

6. 6 x 1

7. 2 x 7

8. 3 x 6

9. 6 x 6

10. 4 x 1

11. 6 x 5

12. 6 x 4

13. 6 x 0

14. 5 x 5

15. 3 x 9

16. 2 x 6

17. 5 x 6

18. 5 x 3

19. 6 x 8

20. 6 x 7

21. 6 x 0

Lesson 8

Multiplication by 7

The answer to a multiplication problem is called the **product**.

Switching the order doesn't matter. The product will always be the same.

7	7	7	7	7	7	7	7	7	7
x 0	x 1	x 2	x 3	x 4	x 5	x 6	x 7	x 8	x 9
0	7	14	21	28	35	42	49	56	63

0	1	2	3	4	5	6	7	8	9
x 7	x 7	x 7	x 7	x 7	x 7	x 7	x 7	x 7	x 7
0	7	14	21	28	35	42	49	56	63

Find the product.

1. 4	**2.** 7	**3.** 4	**4.** 1	**5.** 7	**6.** 2	**7.** 3
x 3	x 0	x 5	x 3	x 6	x 7	x 3
12						

8. 3	**9.** 7	**10.** 3	**11.** 7	**12.** 6	**13.** 1	**14.** 7
x 7	x 9	x 8	x 4	x 5	x 4	x 5

15. 7	**16.** 6	**17.** 7	**18.** 7	**19.** 7	**20.** 1	**21.** 6
x 2	x 7	x 1	x 7	x 8	x 7	x 7

Lesson 9

Multiplication by 8

The answer to a multiplication problem is called the **product**.

Switching the order doesn't matter. The product will always be the same.

8 x 0 = 0	8 x 1 = 8	8 x 2 = 16	8 x 3 = 24	8 x 4 = 32	8 x 5 = 40	8 x 6 = 48	8 x 7 = 56	8 x 8 = 64	8 x 9 = 72
0 x 8 = 0	1 x 8 = 8	2 x 8 = 16	3 x 8 = 24	4 x 8 = 32	5 x 8 = 40	6 x 8 = 48	7 x 8 = 56	8 x 8 = 64	9 x 8 = 72

Find the product.

1. 7 x 8 = 56
2. 4 x 4
3. 8 x 1
4. 2 x 6
5. 0 x 8
6. 7 x 5
7. 9 x 8

8. 3 x 5
9. 3 x 8
10. 6 x 0
11. 8 x 2
12. 5 x 5
13. 2 x 8
14. 8 x 7

15. 5 x 8
16. 8 x 9
17. 8 x 8
18. 4 x 8
19. 8 x 4
20. 5 x 2
21. 3 x 8

Lesson 10

Multiplication by 9

The answer to a multiplication problem is called the **product**.

Switching the order doesn't matter. The product will always be the same.

9	9	9	9	9	9	9	9	9	9
x 0	x 1	x 2	x 3	x 4	x 5	x 6	x 7	x 8	x 9
0	9	18	27	36	45	54	63	72	81

0	1	2	3	4	5	6	7	8	9
x 9	x 9	x 9	x 9	x 9	x 9	x 9	x 9	x 9	x 9
0	9	18	27	36	45	54	63	72	81

Find the product.

1. 9 x 1 = 9
2. 4 x 9
3. 8 x 7
4. 9 x 9
5. 3 x 7
6. 5 x 8
7. 9 x 1
8. 3 x 1
9. 6 x 4
10. 2 x 1
11. 6 x 9
12. 2 x 8
13. 7 x 5
14. 9 x 5
15. 9 x 4
16. 4 x 9
17. 0 x 9
18. 6 x 3
19. 3 x 7
20. 2 x 5
21. 3 x 9

Lesson 11

Multiplication Fill in the Blanks

In multiplication the numbers can be in any order.

Fill in the missing numbers.

1. 3 x 2 = 6
2 x <u>3</u> = 6

2. 4 x 3 = 12
3 x ___ = 12

3. 5 x 4 = 20
4 x ___ = 20

4. 1 x 9 = 9
___ x 1 = 9

5. 6 x 3 = 18
3 x ___ = 18

6. 2 x 5 = 10
5 x ___ = 10

7. 10 x 5 = 50
5 x ___ = 50

8. 8 x 4 = 32
4 x ___ = 32

9. 6 x 6 = 36
___ x 6 = 36

10. 7 x 8 = 56
8 x ___ = 56

Lesson 12

Multiplication by 10

When multiplying a number by 10, multiply the number by one, then bring down the zero.

```
  10              10
 x 8    Then     x 8
 ---             ---
   8              80
```

Solve the problems below.

1. 10 x 3 = 30	**2.** 10 x 2	**3.** 10 x 5	**4.** 10 x 6	**5.** 10 x 1
6. 10 x 5	**7.** 10 x 4	**8.** 10 x 8	**9.** 10 x 7	**10.** 10 x 0
11. 10 x 9	**12.** 10 x 2	**13.** 10 x 4	**14.** 10 x 3	**15.** 10 x 9

Lesson 13

Multiplication by 100

When multiplying a number by 100, multiply the number by one, then bring down the two zeros.

$$\begin{array}{r} 100 \\ \times\ 3 \\ \hline 3 \end{array} \quad \text{Then} \quad \begin{array}{r} 100 \\ \times\ 3 \\ \hline 30 \end{array} \quad \text{Then} \quad \begin{array}{r} 100 \\ \times\ 3 \\ \hline 300 \end{array}$$

Solve the problems below.

1. 100 x 4 = 400

2. 100 x 2

3. 100 x 5

4. 100 x 6

5. 100 x 1

6. 100 x 4

7. 100 x 8

8. 100 x 9

9. 100 x 0

10. 100 x 7

11. 100 x 3

12. 100 x 7

13. 100 x 4

14. 100 x 3

15. 100 x 9

Lesson 14

2-Digit Multiplication

To multiply a two-digit number by a one-digit number, you must first multiply the number in the one's place. Then you multiply the number in the ten's place.

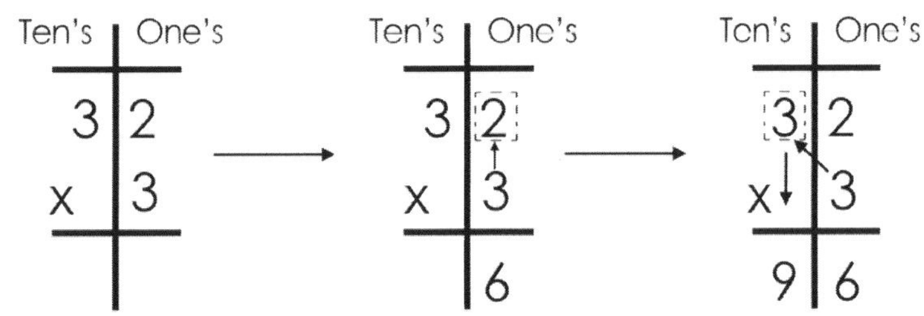

Solve the problems below.

1. 24 x 2 = 48

2. 73 x 3

3. 24 x 5

4. 64 x 2

5. 48 x 1

6. 63 x 1

7. 15 x 5

8. 54 x 2

9. 49 x 1

10. 38 x 2

Chapter 7 - Graphing

Lesson 1

Drawing a Graph 1

Draw a line on the graph to answer each question.

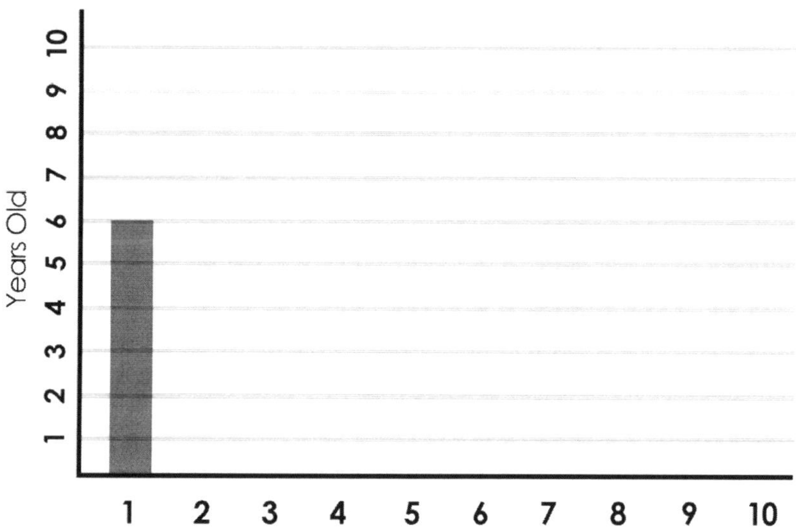

1. Tom is six years old.

2. Laney is seven years old.

3. Jane is two years old.

4. Stan is three years old.

5. Sally is one year old.

6. Mark is ten years old.

7. Mike is four years old.

8. Anne is eight years old.

9. Elle is five years old.

10. Donnie is nine years old.

Drawing a Graph 2

In the chart below color in the boxes on the graph to show your answers for each question.

1. How many pennies equal a nickel?

2. How many nickels equal a dime?

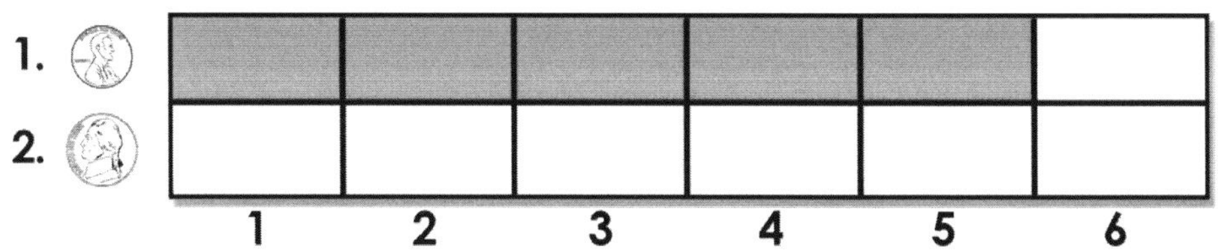

3. How many quarters equal a dollar?

4. How many nickels equal a quarters?

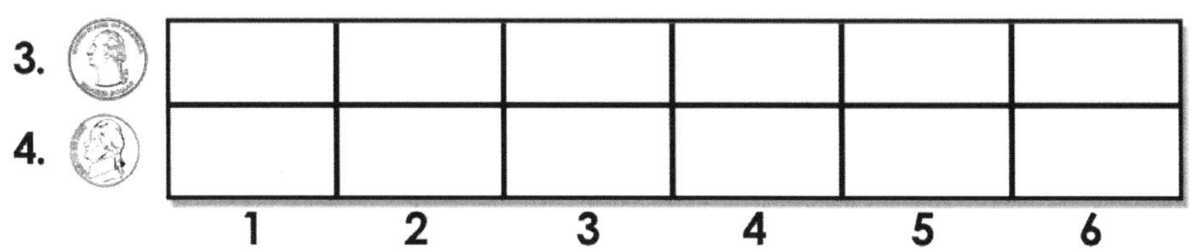

5. How many dimes equal two quarters?

6. How many quarters equal a dollar and a half?

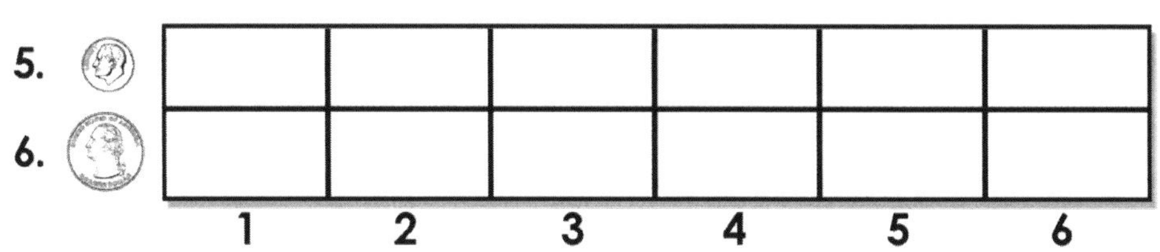

Lesson 2

Reading a Graph

Use the graph to answer the questions.

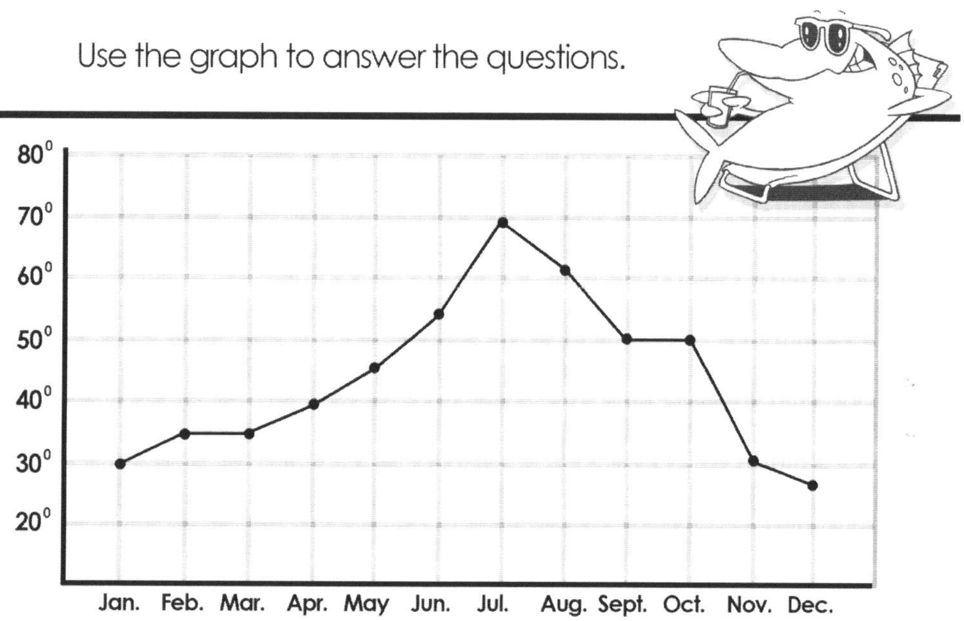

1. What was the coldest month? December

2. What was the hottest month? ______________

3. What was the temperature in March? ______________

4. About how many degrees was the difference between the coldest and hottest months? __________

5. What was the temperature in November? ______________

6. Did it become hotter or colder from April to May? ___________

7. Did the temperature change from September to October? ______________

8. Which month was colder, January or December? ______________

Lesson 3

Reading Pie Charts 1

Foods that families prefer.

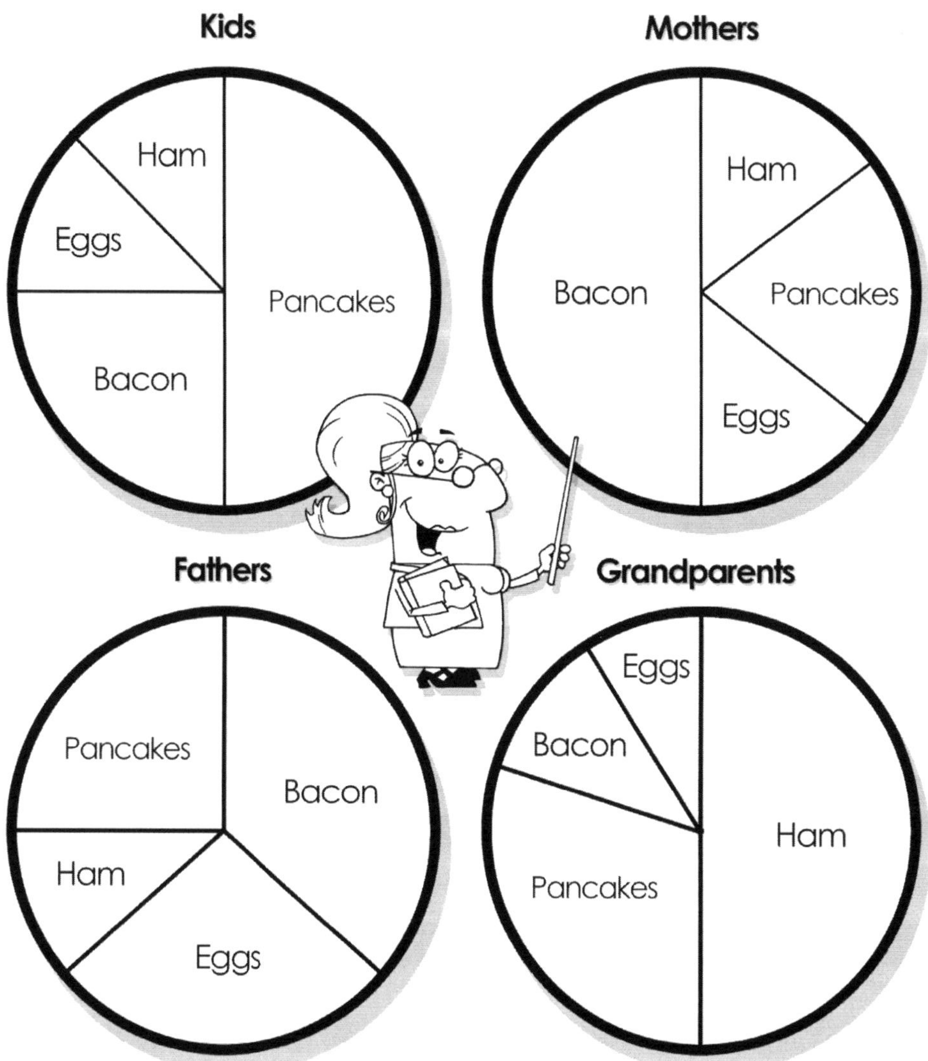

Reading Pie Charts 2

Use the pie charts on the last page to answer the questions below.

1. Which breakfast food do kids like the most ? ____________

2. Which breakfast food do grandparents like the most ? ___________

3. Which breakfast food do mothers like the most? ____________

4. Which breakfast food do fathers like the least? ____________

5. What is the kids' second favorite food ? ____________

6. What is the mothers' second favorite food ? ____________

7. Which breakfast food do grandparents like least ? ____________

Lesson 4

Drawing a Graph 3

Color in a square for each object you see in the picture below.

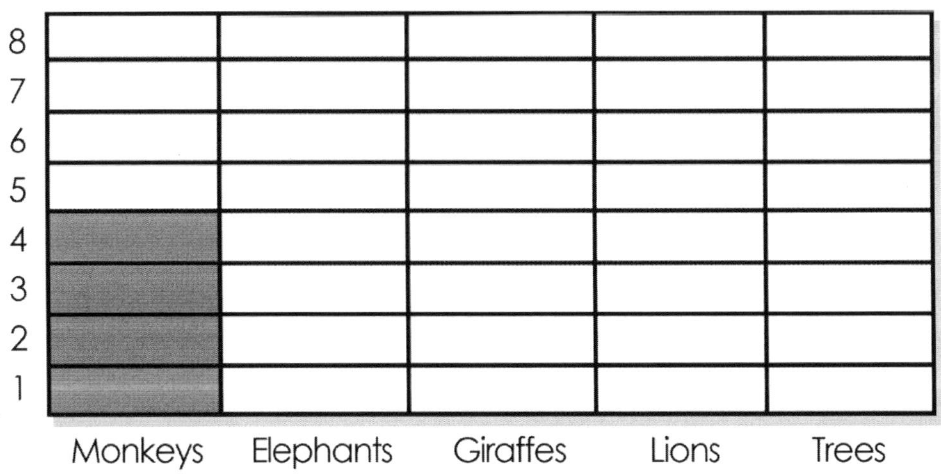

Lesson 4

Drawing a Graph - Matching Questions

Answer the questions using the graph you just made on the last page.

---

1. How many giraffes 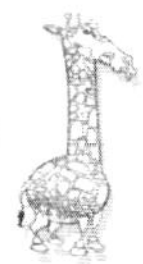 are on the graph ? 3

2. How many elephants  are on the graph ? ________

3. How many lions  are on the graph ? ________

4. How many monkeys  are on the graph ? ________

5. What is the sum of giraffes  and lions  ? ________

6. What is the difference of elephants  and monkeys  ?

____

7. What is the product of lions  times giraffes  ? ________

Lesson 5

Word Problems and Graphs

Answer the questions by completing the chart.

1. Tommy makes $8 a day. He already has $10. How much money will he have in total at the end of the week?

Tommy's Money	Monday	Tuesday	Wednesday	Thursday	Friday	Total
$10	$8	$8	$8	$8	$8	$50

2. Amy has walked 3 miles so far. If she walks 2 miles each day how many miles in total will she have walked at the end of the week?

Amy's Miles	Monday	Tuesday	Wednesday	Thursday	Friday	Total
3	2	2	2	2	2	____

3. Jimmy has 12 pieces of candy. He buys 4 pieces each day. How much candy will he have in total at the end of the week?

Jimmy's Candy	Monday	Tuesday	Wednesday	Thursday	Friday	Total
12	4	4	4	4	4	____

4. Cindy bakes cupcakes. She has 37 so far. She can bake 12 a day. How many will she have in total at the end of the week?

Cindys Cupcakes	Monday	Tuesday	Wednesday	Thursday	Friday	Total
37	12	12	12	12	12	____

Drawing Points on a Graph

Locate the points on the grid and draw the shapes for each question.

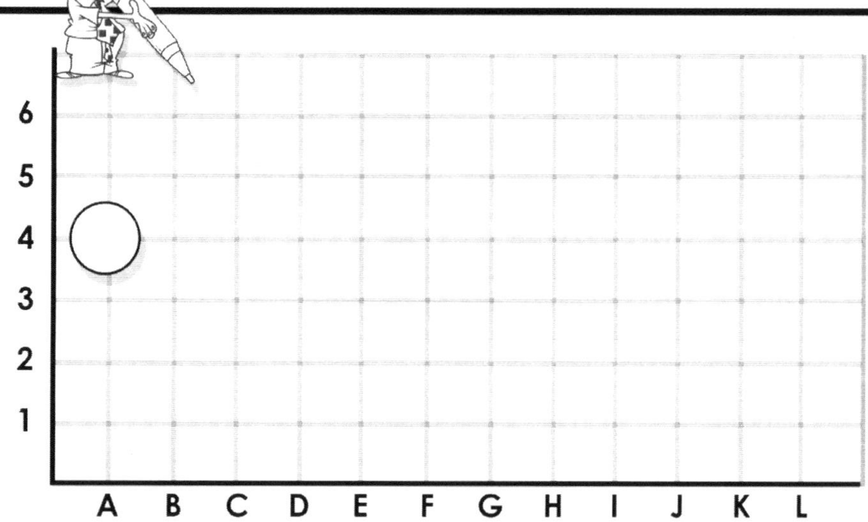

1. A, 4 - 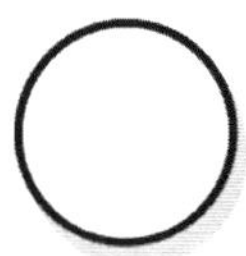

2. C, 1 - 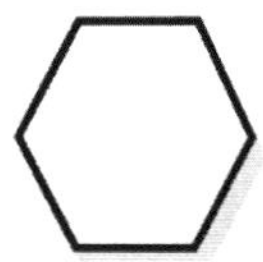

3. K, 6 - 

4. H, 3 - 

5. F, 6 - 

6. L, 1 - 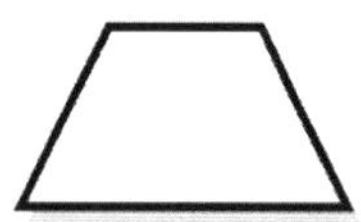

Chapter 8 - Money & Time

Lesson 1

Money: Coins

Each coin has its own value.

= 1 penny = 1¢

= 1 nickel = 5¢

= 1 dime = 10¢

= 1 quarter = 25¢

Lesson 2

Money: Bills

Each bill has its own value.

= One Dollar

= $1

= Five Dollars

= $5

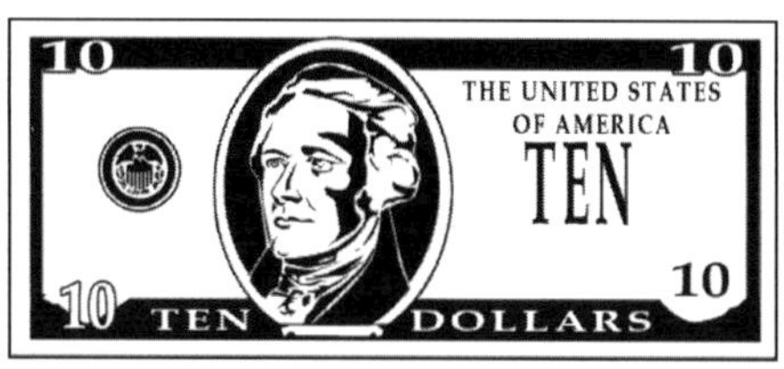

= Ten Dollars

= $10

= Twenty Dollars

= $20

Lesson 3

Counting Money 1

Write the correct amount of money for each question.

1. 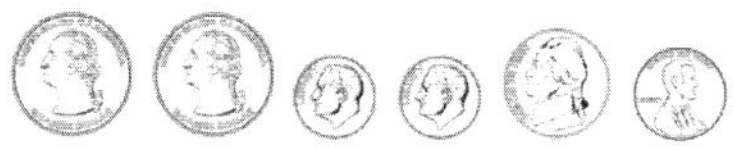 76 ¢

2.  ______¢

3.  $______

4.  $______

5.  ______¢

6.  $______

7.  $______

8.  $______

9. 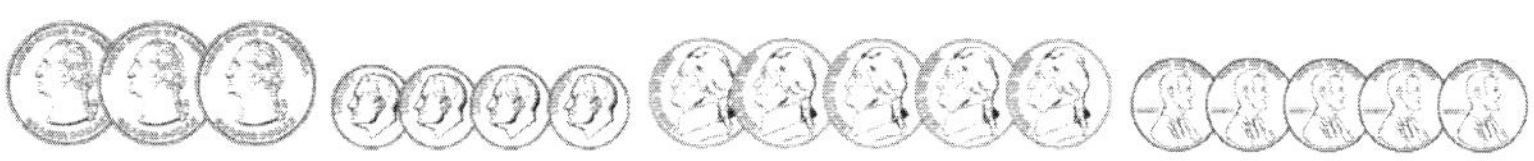 $______

Counting Money 2

Write the correct amount of money for each question.

1. 

$ 1.41

2. 

$______

3. 

$______

4. 

$______

5. 

$______

6. 

$______

Lesson 4

Making Change 1

Write how much change is left over for each question.

1.  = 25 ¢

2.  = ______ ¢

3. 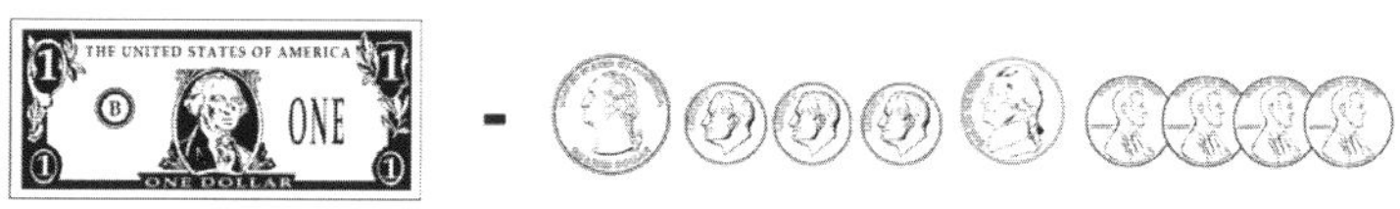 = ______ ¢

4.  = ______ ¢

5.  = $ ______

6.  = $ ______

7.  = $ ______

Lesson 4

Making Change 2

Write how much change is left over for each question.

1.  = $ 3.95

2.  = $______

3.  = $______

4.  = $______

5.  = $______

6.  = $______

7.  = $______

8.  = $______

Lesson 5

Writing Money

Write out each amount.

1. $38.59 = Thirty-eight dollars and fifty-nine cents

2. $100.32 = ______________________

3. $278.12 = ______________________

4. $315.08 = ______________________

5. $915.83 = ______________________

6. $18.33 = ______________________

7. $229.29 = ______________________

8. $756.10 = ______________________

9. $618.24 = ______________________

10. $999.72 = ______________________

Lesson 6

Reading the Clock

The hands of the clock tell us what time it is.

Lesson 7

Time Matching

Draw a line from each clock on the left to match the clock on the right.

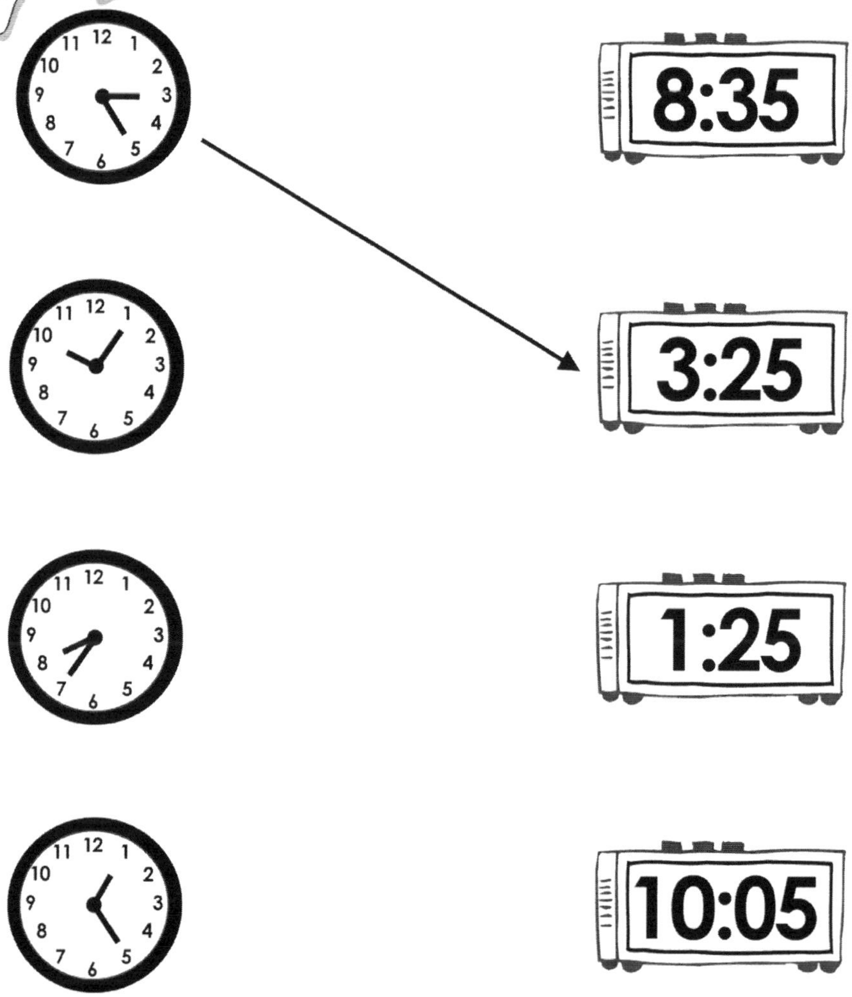

Lesson 8

AM & PM

AM stands for the early hours of the day. It is for the hours between midnight and noon.

PM stands for the later hours of the day. It is for the hours between noon and midnight .

Answer each question with either **AM** or **PM**.

1. Johnny gets on the bus every morning at 7:15 <u>AM</u>.
2. Mary and her family eat dinner every night at 6:30 _____.
3. The sun came up today at 7:00 _____.
4. We eat lunch everyday at 12:15 _____.
5. My favorite cartoon comes on every afternoon at 5:00 _____.
6. Steven wakes up every morning at 6:15 _____.
7. The kids get out of school everyday at 3:15 _____.
8. I go to bed every night at 9:30 _____.
9. Amy eats breakfast every day at 6:30 _____.
10. My sister takes a nap after she eats lunch at 1:00 _____.

Lesson 9

Adding time

Add the hours and minutes together.
(Remember 1 hour = 60 minutes,)

1. 4 hours 15 minutes
\+ 2 hours 30 minutes

6 hours 45 minutes

2. 3 hours 10 minutes
\+ 6 hours 16 minutes

3. 3 hours 5 minutes
\+ 2 hours 7 minutes

4. 9 hours 50 minutes
\+ 6 hours 2 minutes

Subtract the hours and minutes below.
Dont forget to "borrow" from hours when you need to.
(Remember 1 hour = 60 minutes,)

5. 7 hours 30 minutes
\- 3 hours 15 minutes

6. 8 hours 10 minutes
\- 6 hours 16 minutes

7. 3 hours 5 minutes
\- 2 hours 7 minutes

8. 9 hours 50 minutes
\- 6 hours 2 minutes

Lesson 10

Time Passage 1

Write the correct times in the clocks on the right.

What time will it be in 3 hours and 15 minutes?

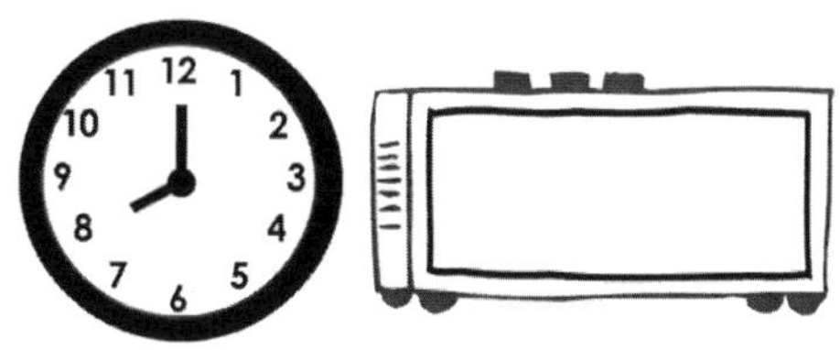

What time will it be in 2 hours and 30 minutes?

What time will it be in 1 hour and 45 minutes?

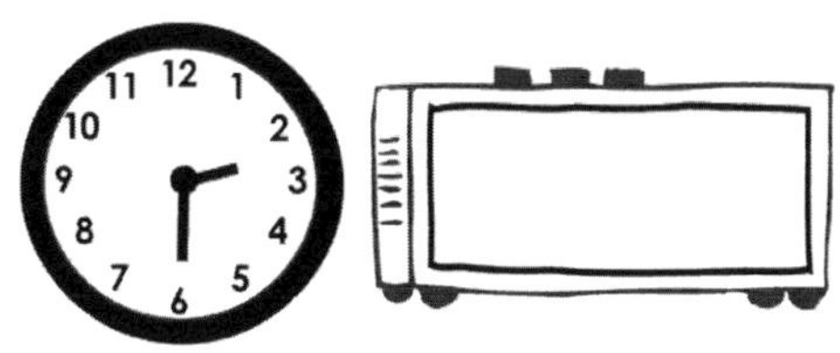

What time will it be in 2 hours and 15 minutes?

What time will it be in 4 hours and 45 minutes?

What time will it be in 3 hours and 30 minutes?

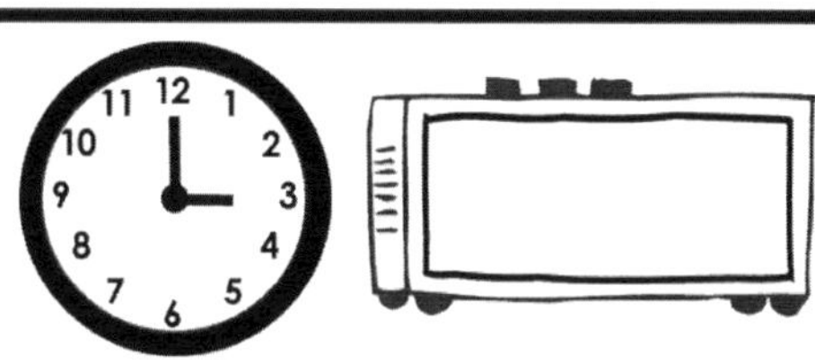

What time will it be in 5 hours and 45 minutes?

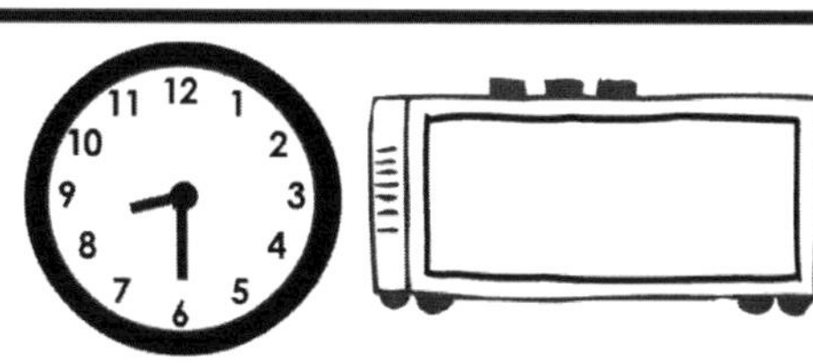

What time will it be in 1 hour and 15 minutes?

Time Passage 2

Draw the hands on the clock to show the proper times.

What time will it be in 2 hours and 20 minutes?

What time will it be in 1 hour and 35 minutes?

What time will it be in 3 hours and 5 minutes?

What time will it be in 6 hours and 10 minutes?

What time will it be in 3 hours and 25 minutes?

What time will it be in 3 hours and 15 minutes?

What time will it be in 5 hours and 35 minutes?

What time will it be in 3 hours and 15 minutes?

Chapter 9 - Geometry & Measurements

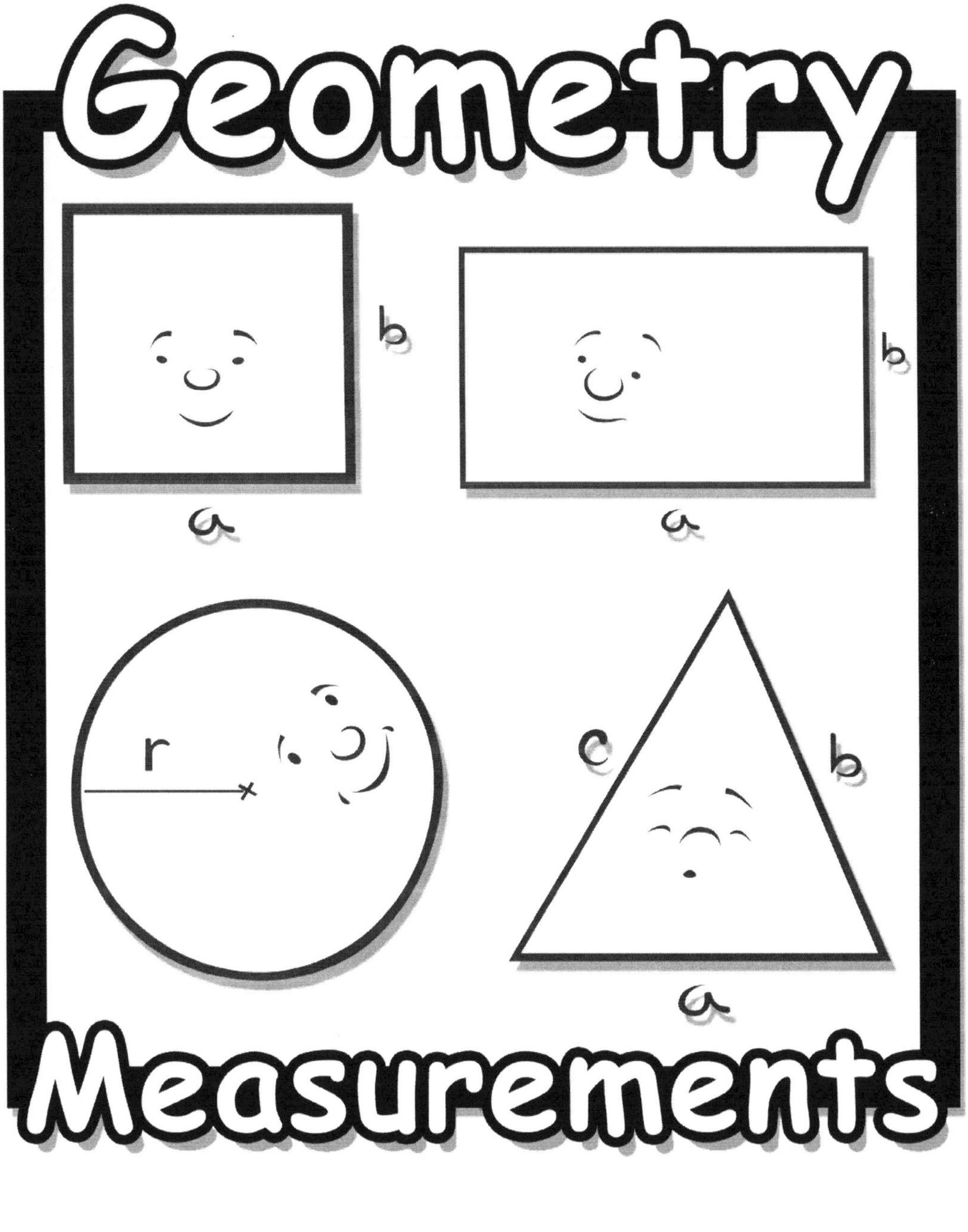

Shapes

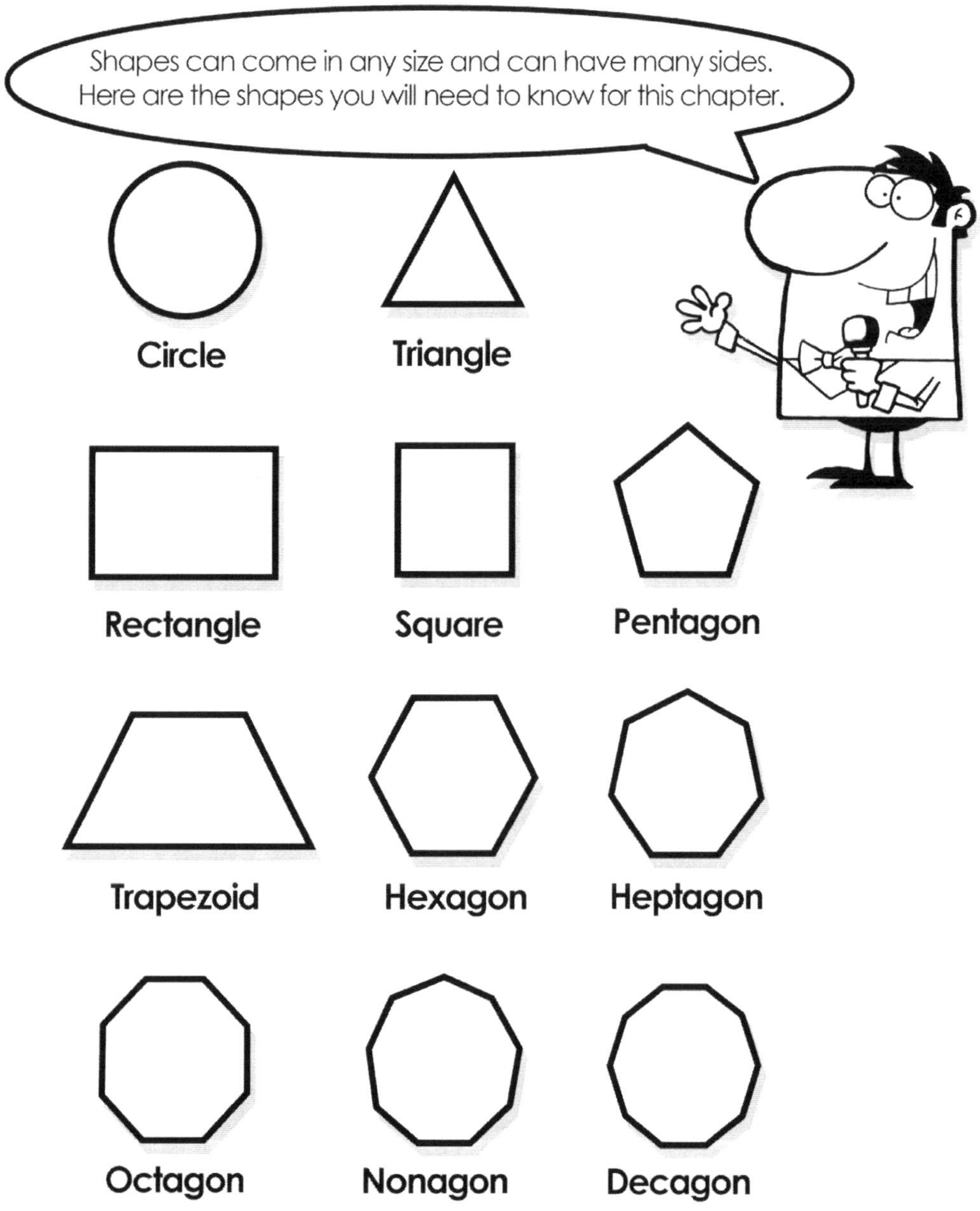
Shapes can come in any size and can have many sides.
Here are the shapes you will need to know for this chapter.
Circle
Triangle
Rectangle
Square
Pentagon
Trapezoid
Hexagon
Heptagon
Octagon
Nonagon
Decagon

Lesson 1

Shape Counting 1

How many smaller shapes can you find in each larger shape? Write your answer.

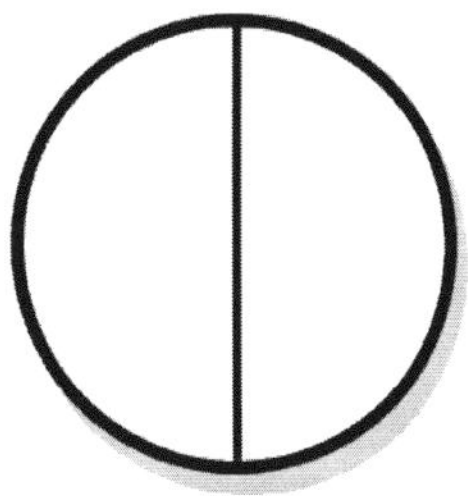 2

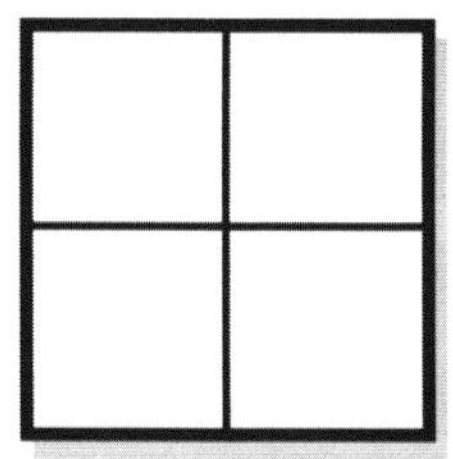 ____

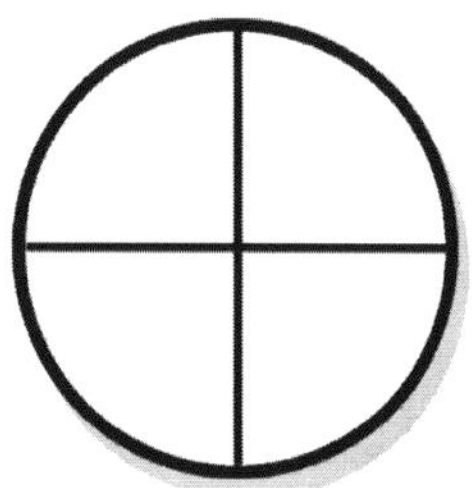 ____

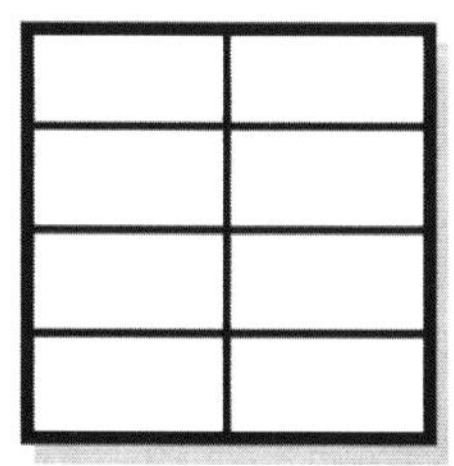 ____

 ____

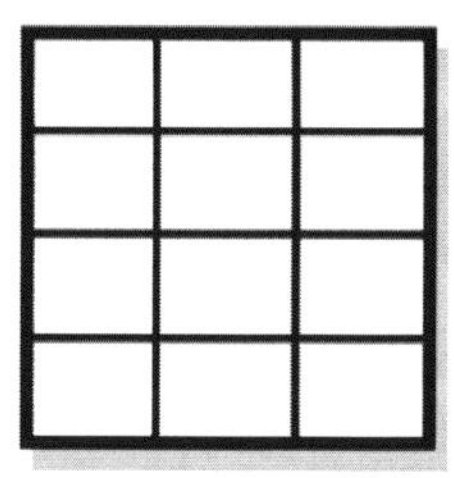 ____

 ____

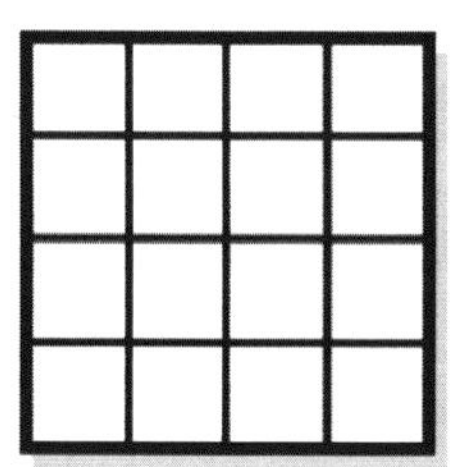 ____

Shape Counting 2

How many smaller shapes can you find in each larger shape? Write your answer.

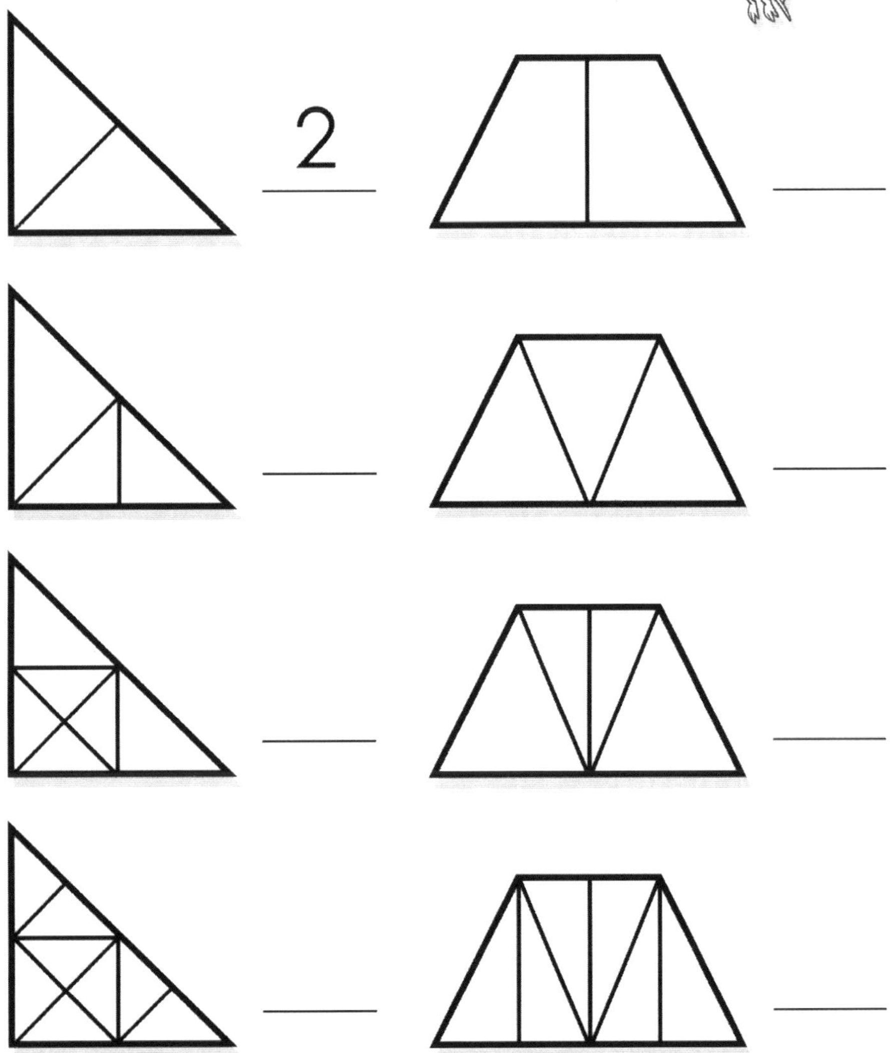

Lesson 2

Comparing Shapes by Sides

Write inside each shape how many sides it has.
Then answer each question.

---

1. 

has how many more sides than 

? 1

---

2. 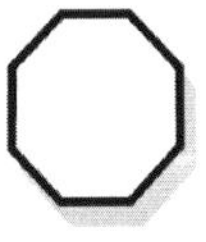 has how many more sides than  ? ______

---

3. How many total sides do you get when you add

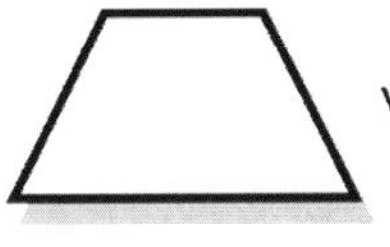 with a 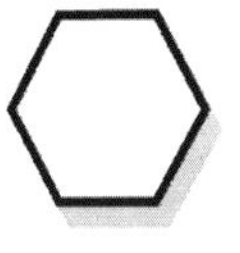 ? ______

---

4. 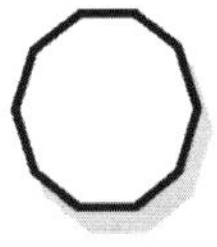 has how many more sides than 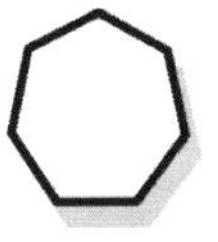 ? ______

---

5. How many total sides do you get when you add

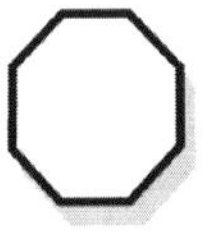 with a  ? ______

Lesson 3

Area 1

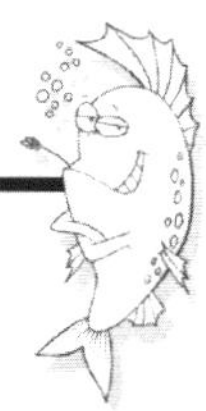

Area is the amount of space inside inside a shape.

Find the area of each shape.

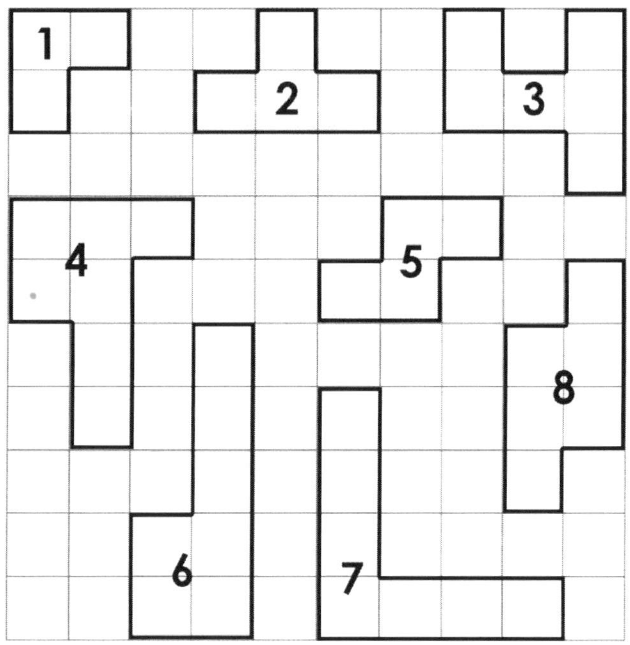

1. 3 Units
2. _____ Units
3. _____ Units
4. _____ Units
5. _____ Units
6. _____ Units
7. _____ Units
8. _____ Units

Area 2

Area is the amount of space inside inside a shape.

Use the grid to draw the shapes for each question.

1. Draw 3 shapes with an area of 2 units each.

2. Draw 2 shapes with an area of 7 units each.

3. Draw 4 shapes with an area of 5 units each.

4. Draw 3 shapes with an area of 9 units each.

5. Draw 2 shapes with an area of 11 units each.

Lesson 4

Perimeter 1

Perimeter is the distance around an object.
Find the perimeter of each object by adding all the sides.
Write out the equation.

1.

4 + 6 + 4 +6 = 20 in.

2.

____

3.

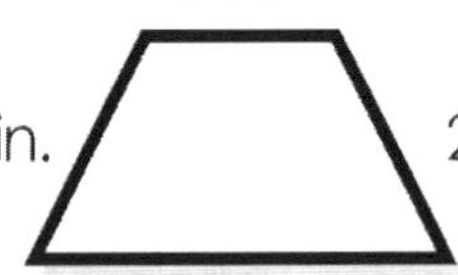

____

4.

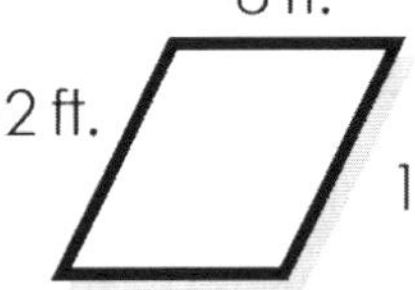

____

5.

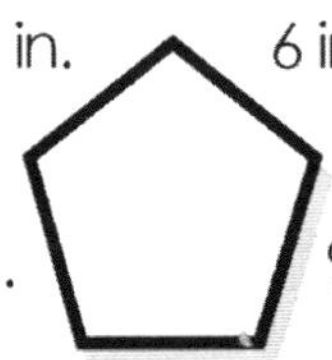

____

6.

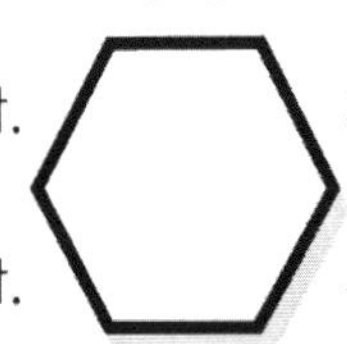

____

Perimeter 2

Perimeter is the distance around a two-dimensional shape.

Find the perimeter of each shape.

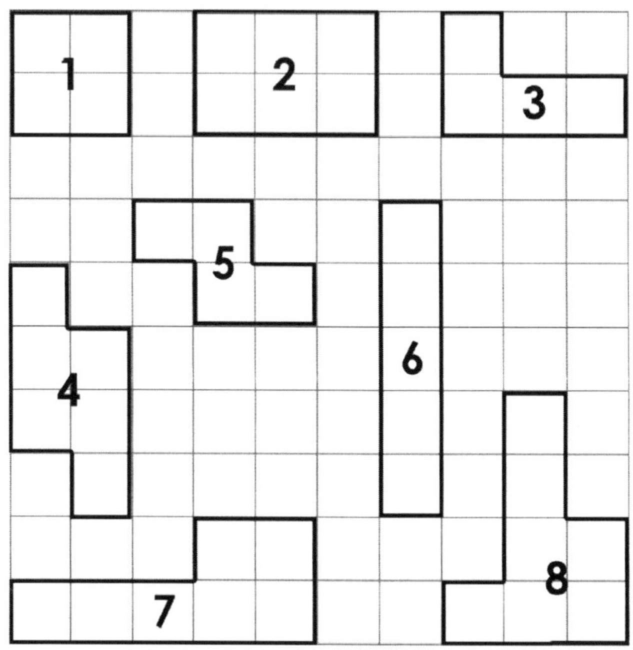

1. 8 Units
2. _____ Units
3. _____ Units
4. _____ Units
5. _____ Units
6. _____ Units
7. _____ Units
8. _____ Units

Perimeter 3

Perimeter is the distance around a two-dimensional shape.

Use the grid to draw the shapes for each question.

1. Draw 3 shapes with a perimeter of 8 units each.

2. Draw 2 shapes with a perimeter of 20 units each.

3. Draw 3 shapes with a perimeter of 12 units each.

4. Draw 1 shape with a perimeter of 14 units.

5. Draw 2 shapes with a perimeter of 16 units each.

Lesson 5

Lines and Line Segments

A point is an exact location in space. •

A line is an endless straight path. ⟷

A line segment is a straight path between two points. A———B

Name if each figure is a point, line or line segment.

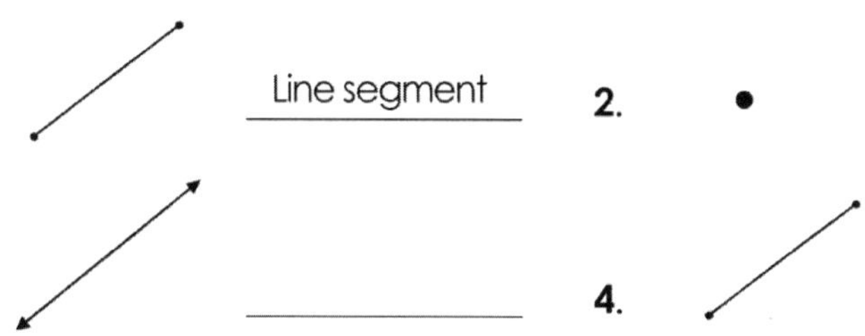

1. Line segment

2. ____________

3. ____________

4. ____________

Use the drawing below to answer the questions.

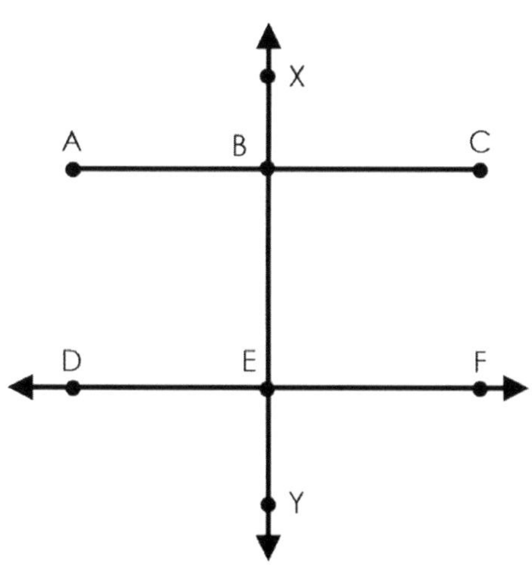

1. Name a line ____________

2. Is AC a line or a line segments?
____

3. Name a point ____________

4. Is DF a line or a line segments?
____

5. At what point does line DF cross line XY? ____________

Lesson 6

Angles

Angles are where two lines meet.

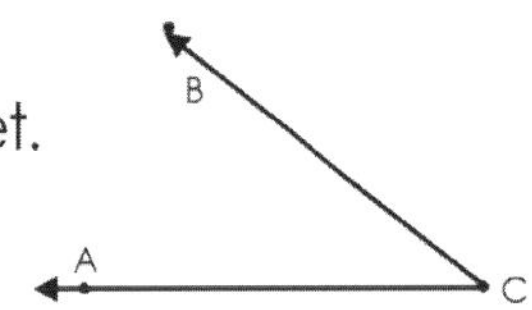

We measure angles in degrees. To write an angle, we use the degree symbol "^{o}". ***Example: 90°***

The measurement of an angle determines its name.

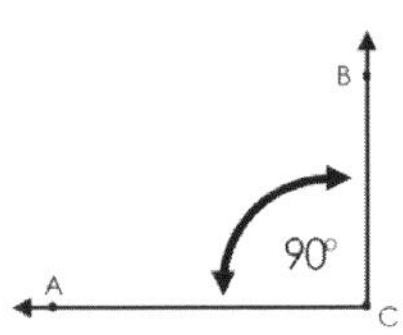	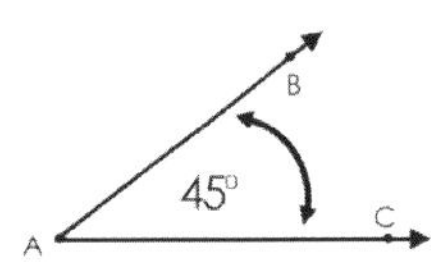	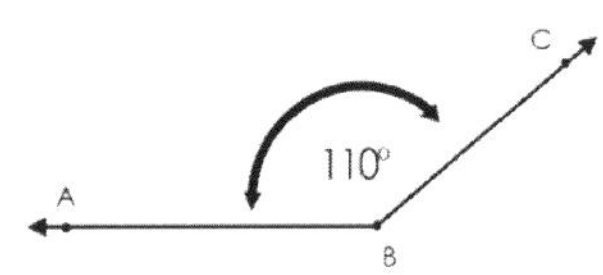
An angle that is exactly 90° is a **right angle**.	An angle that is less than 90° is an **acute angle**.	An angle that is more than 90° is an **obtuse angle**.

Name the types of angles.

1. 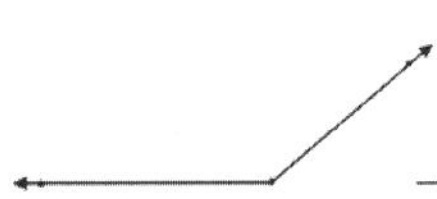 ______________

2. 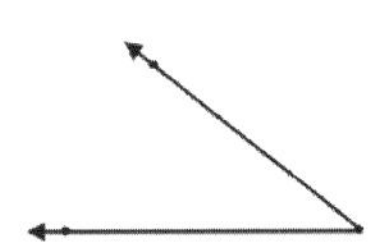 ______________

3. 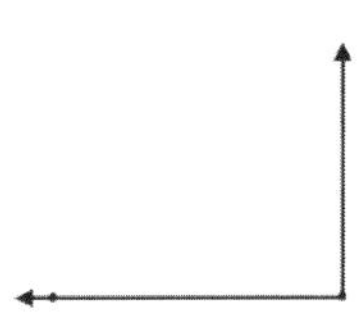 ______________

4. 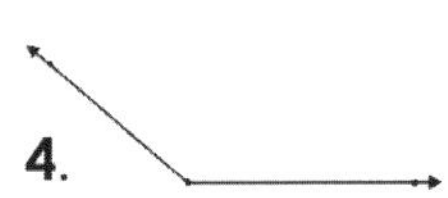 ______________

Lesson 7

Weight Measurements

Two ways weight can be measured is in ounces and pounds.

We use **ounces** to measure the weight of lighter objects. We use **pounds** to measure the weight of heavier objects

 = **9** ounces  = **15** pounds

Circle whether each object should be measured using ounces or pounds.

1. 

Ounces
Pounds

2. 

Ounces
Pounds

3. 

Ounces
Pounds

4. 

Ounces
Pounds

5. 

Ounces
Pounds

6. 

Ounces
Pounds

Lesson 8

Distance Measurements

1 foot = **12** inches
1 yard = **3** feet or **36** inches
1 mile = **1,760** yards

Answer the questions and tell whether each question should use measurement units of a foot, yard or mile

1. The length of a soccer field should be measured in __yards__.
2. Tommys' height should be measured in _________.
3. The distance from home to school is measured in _________.
4. The basketball goal is 10 ________ tall.
5. Steven can jump 3 _________.
6. The distance between the earth and moon is measured in _________.
7. The tree in the yard is 22 ________ tall
8. A football field is measured in _________.
9. Roads are measured in _________.
10. A 12 inch ruler is a _________ long.

Lesson 9

Liquid Measurements

1 Cup	1 Pint	1 Quart	1 Gallon

2 Cups = 1 Pint	2 Pints = 1 Quart	4 Quarts = 1 Gallon

Circle how much liquid each container can hold.

1. 
1 Cup
1 Quart

2. 
1 Cup
1 Gallon

3. 
1 Cup
1 Pint

4. 
1 Quart
1 Cup

5. 
1 Pint
1 Quart

6. 
1 Gallon
1 Cup

Practice Test #1

Practice Questions

1. Jillian writes the number: 860,002. Which of the following represents this number, in words?

Ⓐ Eight hundred sixty thousand, twenty

Ⓑ Eight hundred sixty thousand, two

Ⓒ Eight hundred sixty two thousand

Ⓓ Eight hundred six thousand, two

2. Arlan compares his annual electricity expenses over a five-year time span. His annual expenses are shown in the table below.

Year	Expense
2007	$1,224
2008	$1,319
2009	$1,046
2010	$1,529
2011	$1,342

Which of the following shows the years listed, in order, from lowest electricity expense to highest electricity expense?

Ⓐ 2009, 2008, 2007, 2010, 2011

Ⓑ 2007, 2009, 2011, 2010, 2008

Ⓒ 2009, 2007, 2011, 2008, 2010

Ⓓ 2009, 2007, 2008, 2011, 2010

3. Steve had to pay a library fee. The amount he paid is shown below.

How much did he pay?

Ⓐ $2.84

Ⓑ $2.59

Ⓒ $2.74

Ⓓ $2.69

4. Wyatt's coach passed out balls to the entire team. One-third of the balls Wyatt received were basketballs. Which of the following could represent the balls he received?

Ⓐ 

Ⓑ 

Ⓒ 

Ⓓ 

5. What number sentence is illustrated by the diagram below?

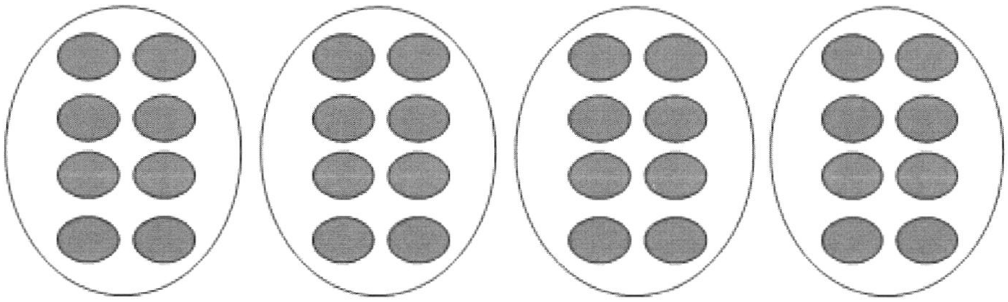

Ⓐ $32 \times 4 = 128$

Ⓑ $32 - 4 = 28$

Ⓒ $32 \div 4 = 8$

Ⓓ $32 + 4 = 36$

6. Which three statements below can be represented by the expression 6×5?
Circle the correct answers.

I. A student has 6 pieces of gum and 5 pieces of candy.
II. A teacher gives 6 students 5 books each.
III. There are 5 students playing on the playground and 6 more join them.
IV. There are 6 cars and each one is carrying 5 people.
V. There are 5 rows of chairs in the auditorium with 6 chairs per row.

7. Edward ascends to the top of a mountain over the course of two days. On Friday, he ascends 482 feet. He ascends another 362 feet on Saturday. How many feet did he ascend in all?

Ⓐ 848 feet

Ⓑ 836 feet

Ⓒ 840 feet

Ⓓ 844 feet

8. Kristen must buy three items that are priced at \$4.58, \$6.22, and \$8.94. What is the best estimate for the total cost of all three items?

Ⓐ \$18

Ⓑ \$16

Ⓒ \$20

Ⓓ \$22

9. Which of the following represents $\frac{2}{3}$?

Ⓐ 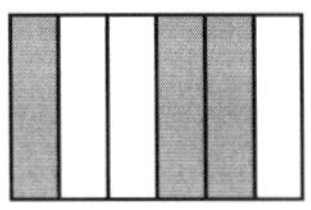

Ⓑ 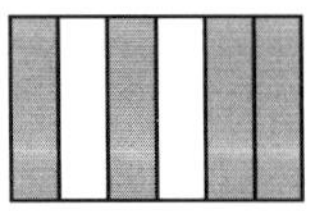

Ⓒ 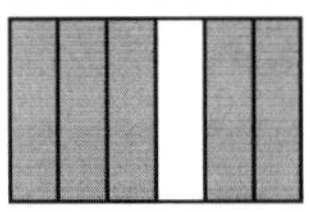

Ⓓ 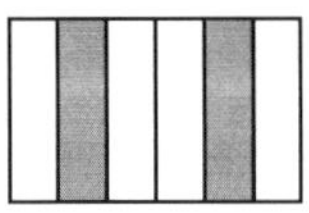

10. On Monday, David finished gluing 96 tiles in 8 hours. On Tuesday, he finished gluing 72 tiles in 8 hours. Which of the following is a possible first step in determining how many more tiles he glued per hour on Monday?

Ⓐ Add the number of tiles glued each day

Ⓑ Subtract the number of hours it took to glue the tiles from the number of tiles glued

Ⓒ Multiply the number of hours spent gluing tiles on Monday by the number of hours spent gluing tiles on Tuesday

Ⓓ Divide the number of tiles glued each day by the number of hours it took to glue them

11. At the birthday party, each guest received 12 game tokens and each game takes 2 tokens. If there were 8 guests at the party, how many tokens were given out?

____

Part B: How many games were played?

____

12. A little boy has three nickels, four dimes, two pennies, and two quarters. How much money does he have?

Ⓐ \$1.00

Ⓑ \$0.90

Ⓒ \$1.07

Ⓓ \$100

13. James drew the following connected squares and labeled them as Figure 1, Figure 2, and so on.

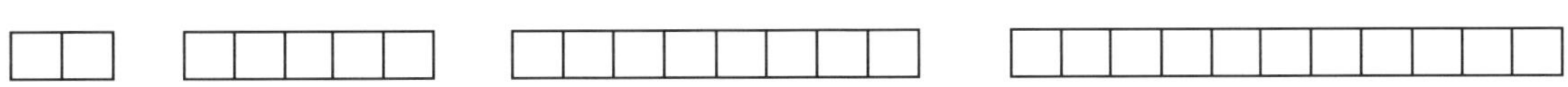

Figure 1 Figure 2 Figure 3 Figure 4

If he continues this pattern, how many squares will he use for Figure 9?

Ⓐ 21

Ⓑ 23

Ⓒ 26

Ⓓ 29

14. A teacher donates to a local charity. Each year, she donates three times the amount donated the previous year. If the teacher donated $2 the first year, how much did she donate during the fifth year?

Ⓐ $158

Ⓑ $164

Ⓒ $162

Ⓓ $144

15. Fill in the blanks below to complete the equation.

$\_\_ \times 3 = 12$

$16 - \_\_ = 10$

$8 + \_\_ = 17$

16. A class collects spiders. Spiders have 8 legs each. Which table shows the number of legs found on the spiders brought to class?

Ⓐ

Number of Spiders	Number of Legs
2	10
3	11
6	14
8	16
11	19

Ⓑ

Number of Spiders	Number of Legs
4	28
5	35
9	63
12	84
14	98

Ⓒ

Number of Spiders	Number of Legs
3	12
4	13
8	17
10	19
12	21

Ⓓ

Number of Spiders	Number of Legs
3	24
5	40
6	48
9	72
12	96

17. The total number of candy pieces found in different numbers of candy jars is shown in the table below.

Number of Candy Jars	Number of Candy Pieces
2	28
4	56
5	70
9	126

How many candy pieces are there in 13 candy jars?

Ⓐ 154

Ⓑ 168

Ⓒ 182

Ⓓ 196

18. Penny drinks 8 glasses of water each day. The number of glasses of water she drinks over a 12-day time span can be determined, using the number sentence: $8 \times 12 = ?$
Which number sentence would not show the number of glasses of water she drinks?

Ⓐ $? \div 8 = 12$

Ⓑ $12 \times 8 = ?$

Ⓒ $? \div 12 = 8$

Ⓓ $12 - 8 = ?$

19. Belinda draws a rectangle with a length of 6 cm and a width of 2 cm. She draws a second rectangle with a length of 9 cm and a width of 5 cm, and she draws a third rectangle with a length of 7 cm and a width of 3 cm. Draw a line to match the rectangle with its correct area.

45 Sq. Ft.	Rectangle 1
18 Sq. Ft.	
21 Sq. Ft.	Rectangle 2
12 Sq. Ft.	
35 Sq. Ft.	Rectangle 3

20. Which of the following figures is NOT congruent to the others shown?

Ⓐ 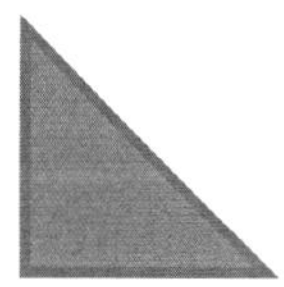

Ⓑ 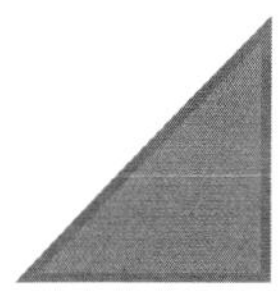

Ⓒ 

Ⓓ 

21. Which number is greater than the number shown by Point M on the number line?

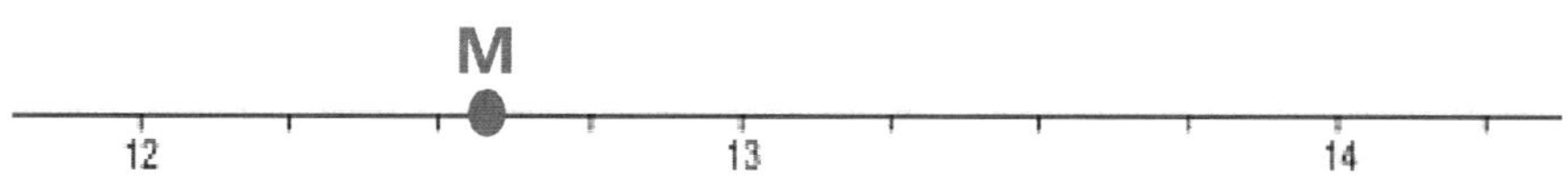

Ⓐ 12 ¼

Ⓑ 12 ½

Ⓒ 12

Ⓓ 12 ¾

22. Which figure has more than 9 edges?

Ⓐ 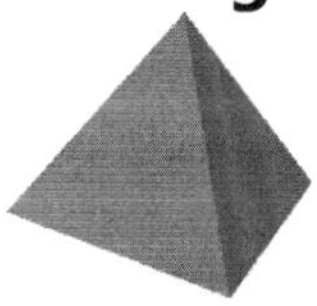

Ⓑ 

Ⓒ 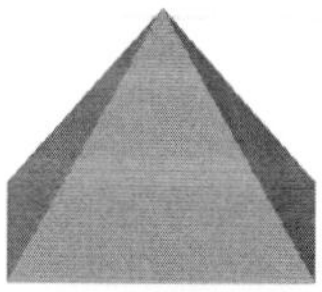

Ⓓ 

23. Which shape has a number of vertices that is equal to two times the number of vertices found on a triangle?

Ⓐ 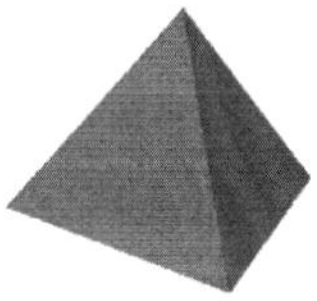

Ⓑ 

Ⓒ 

Ⓓ 

24. Which of the following shapes has 6 faces? Select all that apply.

I. Square pyramid
II. Triangular prism
III. Cube
IV. Triangular pyramid
V. Rectangular prism

25. Which of the following is congruent to the shape shown below?

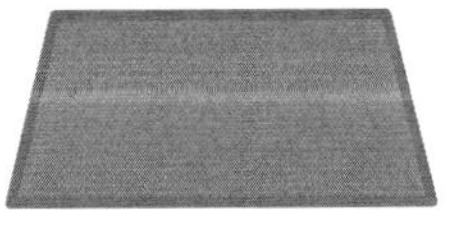

Ⓐ

Ⓑ

Ⓒ

Ⓓ

26. Part A: What number does Point P represent?

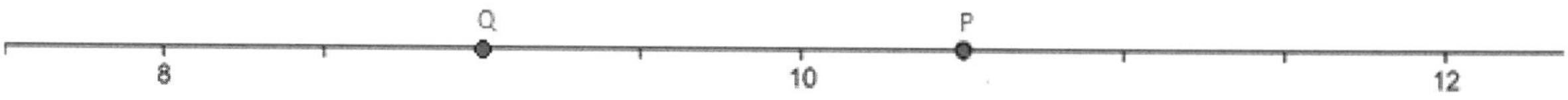

Ⓐ $10\frac{1}{4}$

Ⓑ $10\frac{1}{2}$

Ⓒ $10\frac{1}{3}$

Ⓓ $10\frac{3}{4}$

Part B: How much bigger is the number represented by point P than the number represented by Point Q?

Ⓐ $1\frac{1}{2}$

Ⓑ $\frac{2}{3}$

Ⓒ 1

Ⓓ $\frac{3}{4}$

27. Which of the following shapes has 5 fewer lines of symmetry than an octagon?

Ⓐ 

Ⓑ 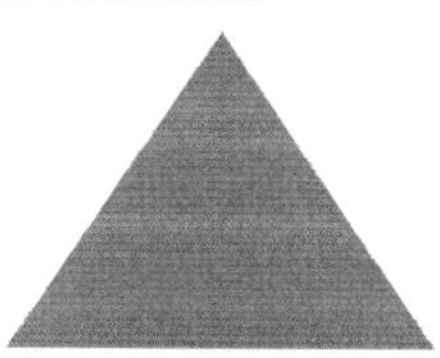

Ⓒ 

Ⓓ 

28. What is the perimeter of the figure shown below?

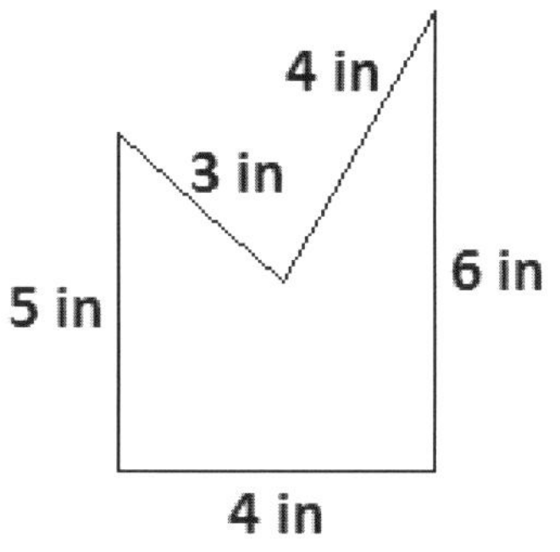

Ⓐ 20 in

Ⓑ 22 in

Ⓒ 24 in

Ⓓ 21 in

29. What is the perimeter of the trapezoid shown below?

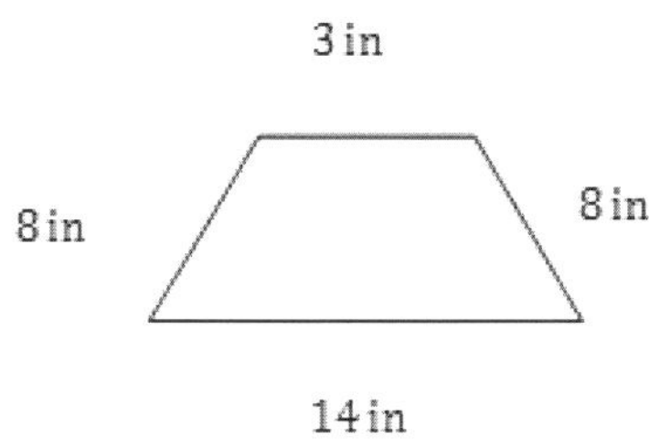

Ⓐ 28 in

Ⓑ 31 in

Ⓒ 34 in

Ⓓ 33 in

30. The rectangle below has a length that is three times its width. What is the length of this rectangle?

Ⓐ 10 in

Ⓑ 14 in

Ⓒ 18 in

Ⓓ 20 in

31. How many square units are found in the trapezoid below?

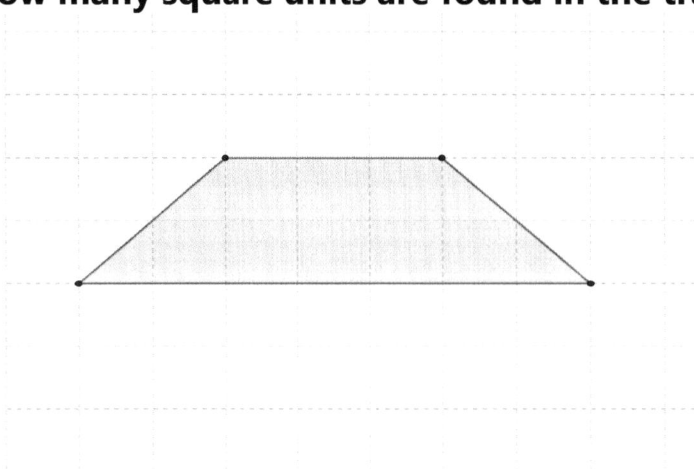

Ⓐ 8 square units

Ⓑ 12 square units

Ⓒ 10 square units

Ⓓ 9 square units

32.

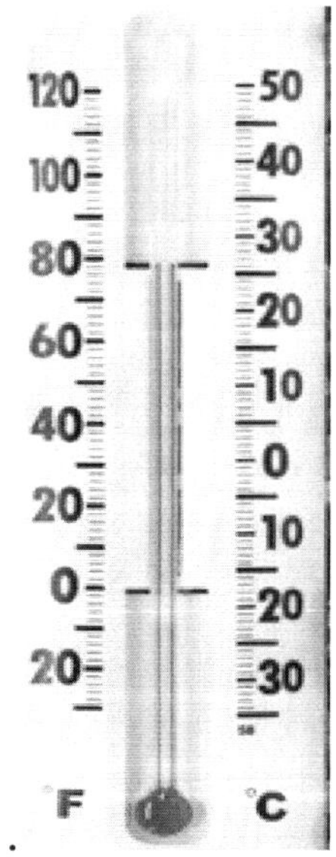

What is the approximate temperature, in degrees Fahrenheit?

Ⓐ 0° F

Ⓑ 80° F

Ⓒ 30° F

Ⓓ 25° F

33. Karen goes to the library at the time shown on the clock below. At what time does she go to the library?

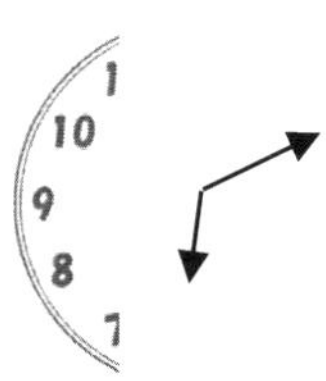

Ⓐ 8:10

Ⓑ 1:30

Ⓒ 6:10

Ⓓ 2:30

34. Which of the figures below is shaded to represent $\frac{5}{8}$?

Ⓐ 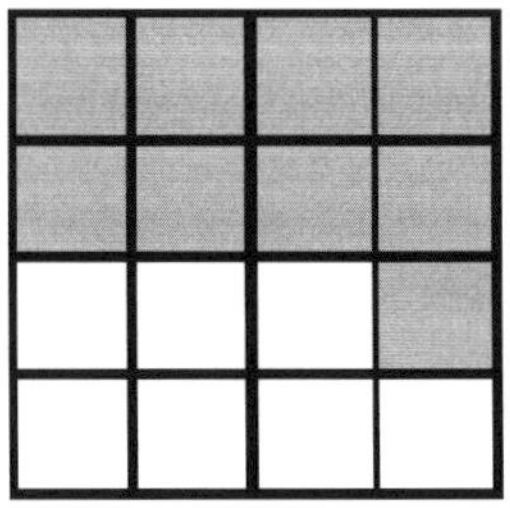

Ⓑ 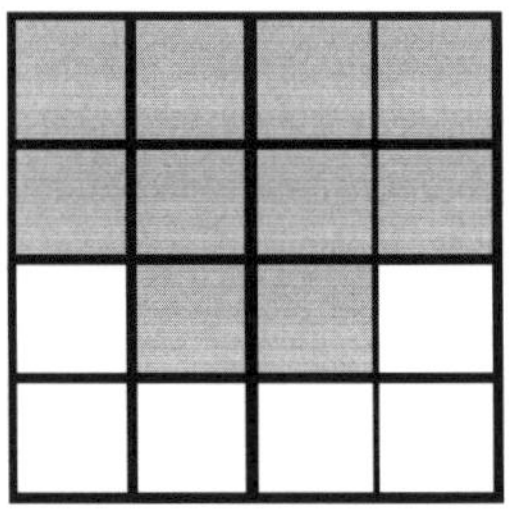

Ⓒ 

Ⓓ 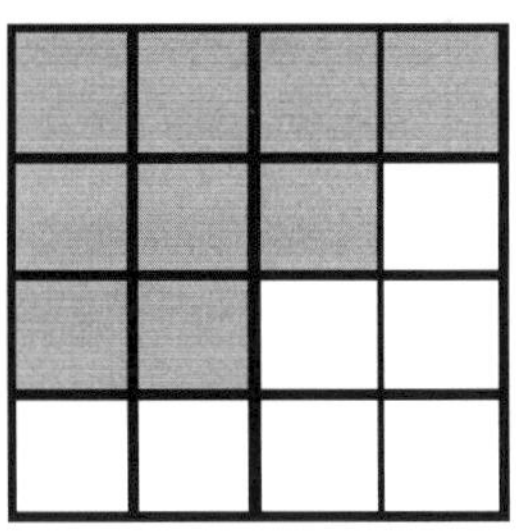

35. To get ready for school in the morning Ashley does the following:

- **Takes 6 minutes to get dressed**
- **Takes 7 minutes to fix her hair**
- **Takes 12 minutes to eat breakfast**
- **Brushes her teeth for 2 minutes**

What is the total time it takes her to get ready for school in the morning?

____

36. The bar graph below shows the number of zoos found in four states.

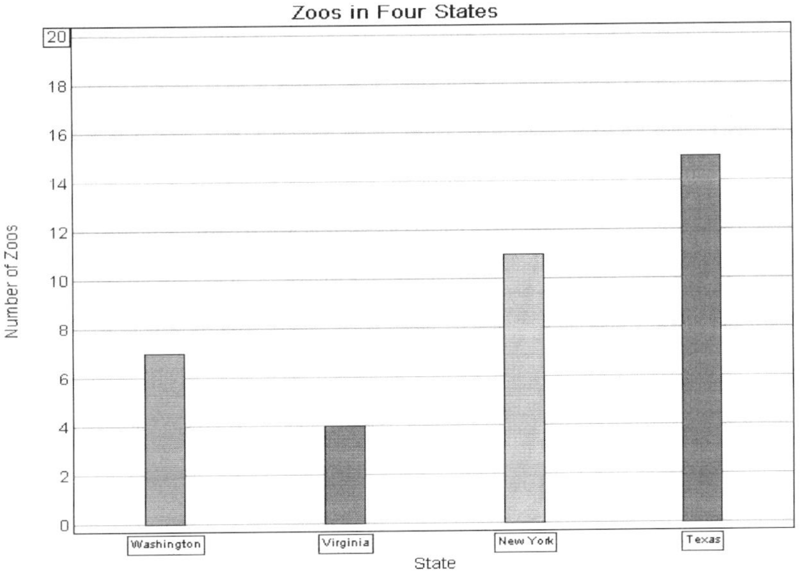

Which state has the most zoos?

Ⓐ Washington

Ⓑ Virginia

Ⓒ New York

Ⓓ Texas

37. A fish bowl contains 2 striped, 4 orange, and 2 blue fish. Eli randomly scoops a fish from the bowl. Which of the following statements is true?

Ⓐ He is less likely to scoop an orange than a striped fish

Ⓑ He is more likely to scoop a striped than a blue fish

Ⓒ He is more likely to scoop a blue than an orange fish

Ⓓ He is equally likely to scoop a striped and a blue fish

38. Which expression below has the same value as $23 + 48 + 32$?

Ⓐ $20 + 40 + 32 + 2 + 3 + 8$

Ⓑ $3 + 8 + 2 + 4 + 2 + 3$

Ⓒ $20 + 40 + 30 + 3 + 2 + 4 + 8$

Ⓓ $40 + 20 + 30 + 3 + 8 + 2$

39. The bar graph below shows the favorite sport of the students in the class.

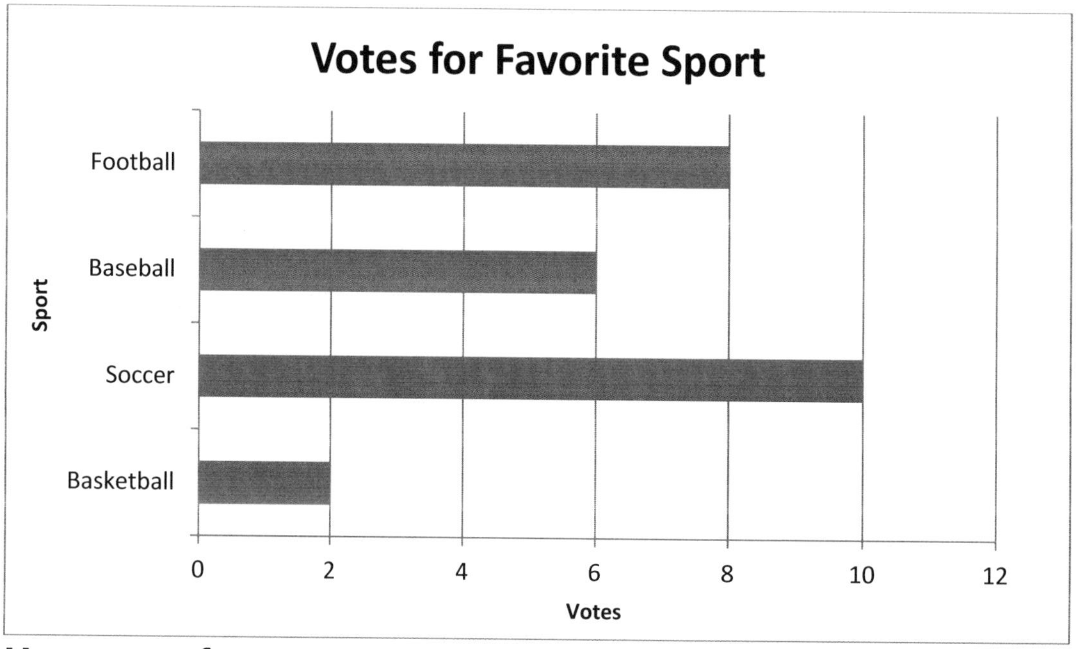

How many fewer votes did basketball get compared to baseball?

Ⓐ 2

Ⓑ 3

Ⓒ 4

Ⓓ 5

40. The number of lawns, finished by four different landscaping companies, in one week, is shown in the table below.

Landscaping Company	Number of Lawns
Landscaping Company A	12
Landscaping Company B	18
Landscaping Company C	6
Landscaping Company D	16

Which pictograph shows the number of lawns finished by each company?

Ⓐ

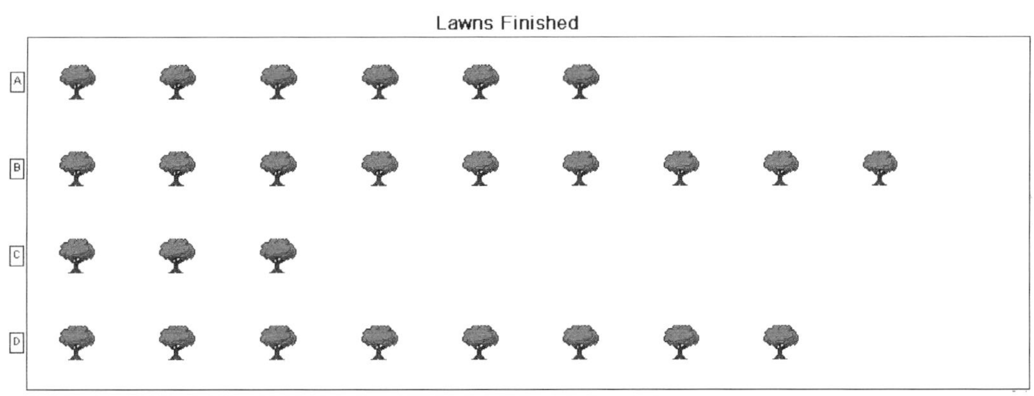

Each tree represents 2 lawns.

Ⓑ

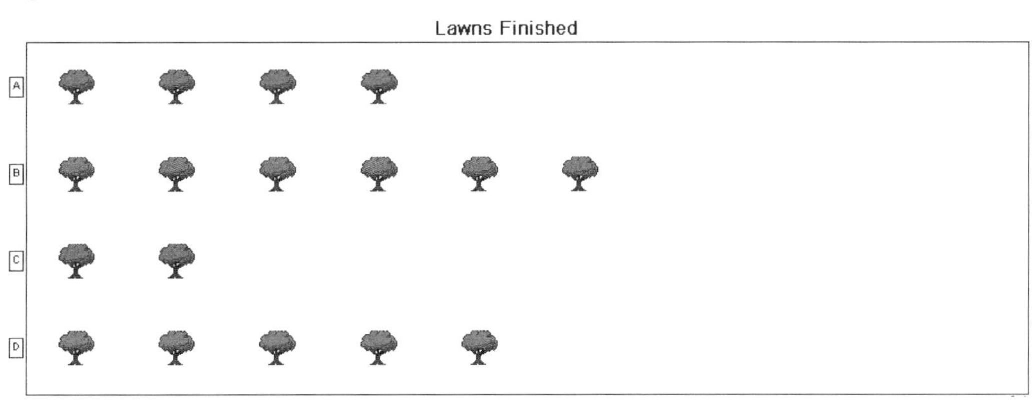

Each tree represents 4 lawns.

Ⓒ

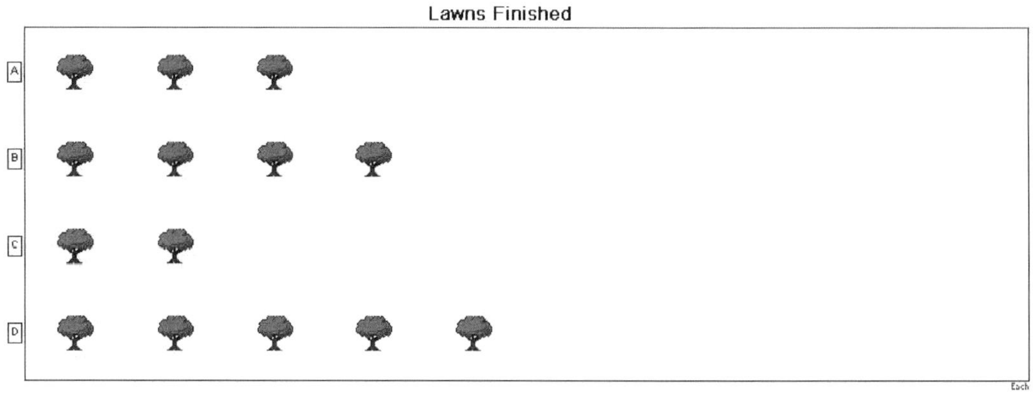

Each tree represents 2 lawns.

Ⓓ

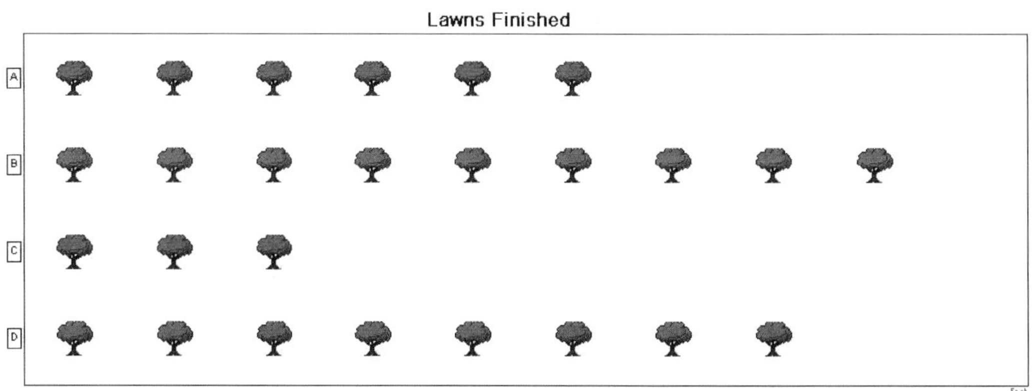

Each tree represents 3 lawns.

Practice Test #2

Practice Questions

1. Which of the following is an expression for five subtracted from twenty-five equals twenty?

Ⓐ 25 - 20 = 5

Ⓑ 5 - 25 = 5

Ⓒ 25 - 5 = 20

Ⓓ 20 + 5 = 25

2. Camille's teacher passed out crayons and pencils to students in her class. One-fourth of the writing tools Camille received were crayons. Which of the following could represent the number of crayons she received?

Ⓐ 

Ⓑ 

Ⓒ 

Ⓓ 

3. Bercu sells 128 hot dogs this month. She sold 117 hot dogs last month. How many hot dogs has she sold in these past two months?

Ⓐ 235

Ⓑ 241

Ⓒ 242

Ⓓ 245

4. What number sentence is shown by the diagram below?

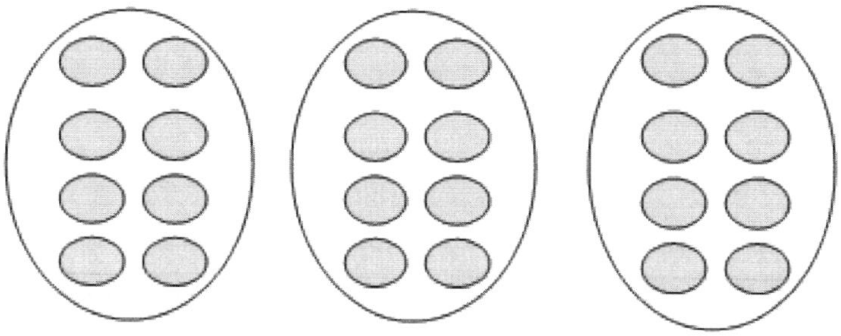

Ⓐ $24 \times 3 = 72$

Ⓑ $24 - 8 = 16$

Ⓒ $24 + 8 = 32$

Ⓓ $24 \div 3 = 8$

5. Which of the following answers are the same as 6×8? Select all that apply.

I. $2 \times 3 \times 8$
II. 6 groups of 8 apples
III. $4 \times 2 \times 8$
IV. 8 people join another group of 6 people
V. 6 people each have 8 t-shirts

6. Fill in the blanks to complete the equation.

$\mathbf{7} \times$ __ $= \mathbf{28}$

__ $+ \mathbf{9} = \mathbf{22}$

$\mathbf{18} -$ __ $= \mathbf{5}$

7. Farm A has 8 chickens and 3 horses. Farm B has 6 chickens and 5 horses. Which of the following is a possible first step in determining which farm contains more animal feet?

Ⓐ Multiply the number of chickens on each farm by 2, and multiply the number of horses on each farm by 4

Ⓑ Find the total number of animals found on both farms

Ⓒ Multiply the sum of the number of chickens and horses, found on both farms, by 6

Ⓓ Add 2 to the number of chickens found on each farm, and add 4 to the number of horses found on each farm

8. Which model shows a fraction that is more than 4 out of 7?

Ⓐ 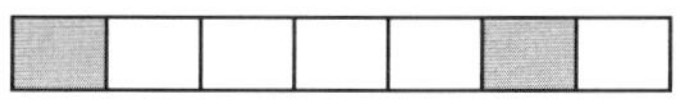

Ⓑ 

Ⓒ 

Ⓓ 

9. The number of miles Jacob has walked each year over the past five years is shown in the table below.

Year 1	691
Year 2	567
Year 3	144
Year 4	963
Year 5	221

Which sequence of years shows the number of miles he walked each year, listed in order from greatest to least?

Ⓐ Year 2, Year 4, Year 5, Year 1, Year 3

Ⓑ Year 4, Year 1, Year 2, Year 5, Year 3

Ⓒ Year 1, Year 4, Year 2, Year 5, Year 3

Ⓓ Year 3, Year 2, Year 5, Year 4, Year 1

10. A neighborhood contains 4 streets. Street 1 has 23 houses, Street 2 has 12 houses, and Street 3 has 34 houses. Estimate by rounding, how many houses are in this neighborhood?

Ⓐ 40

Ⓑ 50

Ⓒ 60

Ⓓ 70

11. Which of the following fraction is equal to $\frac{2}{3}$? Select all that apply.

I. $\frac{4}{6}$

II. $\frac{9}{12}$

III. $\frac{4}{10}$

IV. $\frac{10}{15}$

V. $\frac{6}{10}$

12. Which of the following fractions are bigger than $\frac{5}{8}$?

I. $\frac{5}{9}$

II. $\frac{5}{6}$

III. $\frac{3}{4}$

IV. $\frac{1}{2}$

V. $\frac{4}{10}$

13. A farmer plants rows of corn each growing season. The table below shows the total number of rows of corn the farmer has planted after several seasons.

Season	Number of Rows
Season 2	34
Season 4	68
Season 6	102
Season 7	119
Season 10	

How many rows of corn will the farmer have planted by the end of Season 10?

Ⓐ 153

Ⓑ 170

Ⓒ 136

Ⓓ 168

14. What is the area of the figure shown below?

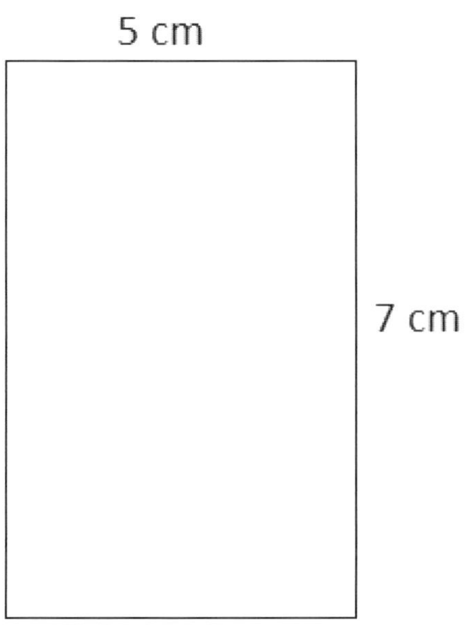

15. Anand has 45 stamps in his collection. He decides to give all of his stamps to 5 friends. He writes the number sentence below to find out how many stamps to give each friend, if each friend is to receive an equal amount.

$$45 \div 5 = ?$$

Which number sentence would NOT help him find the number of stamps to give each friend?

Ⓐ $? \times 5 = 45$

Ⓑ $45 - 5 = ?$

Ⓒ $45 \div ? = 5$

Ⓓ $5 \times ? = 45$

16. The table below shows the number of books students brought to share with the class.

Number of Students	Number of Books
2	8
5	20
6	24
8	32

How many books did 12 students bring?

Ⓐ 44

Ⓑ 36

Ⓒ 40

Ⓓ 48

17. Which figure has 6 vertices?

Ⓐ 

Ⓑ 

Ⓒ 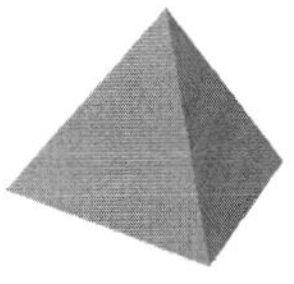

Ⓓ 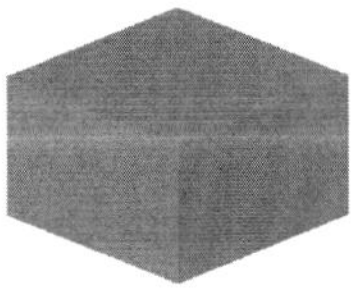

18. Which shape has more lines of symmetry than the one shown below?

Ⓐ 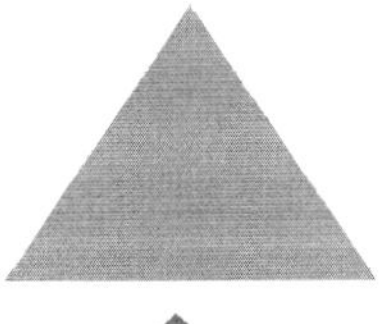

Ⓑ 

Ⓒ 

Ⓓ 

19. Plot a point on the number line below that represents $14\frac{1}{2}$.

20. What statement is NOT true about the figure below?

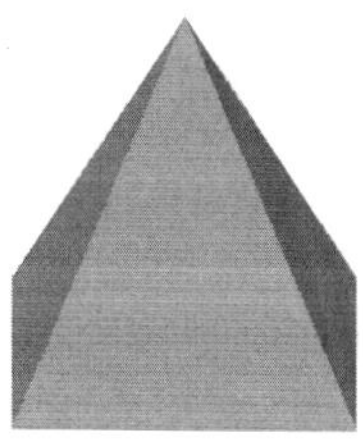

Ⓐ It has 5 vertices

Ⓑ It has 6 edges

Ⓒ It is a pyramid

Ⓓ It has 5 faces

21. Kerrie has 152 stickers. She decides to give 34 of them away to friends. Then she goes to the store and buys 67 more stamps. How many stamps does she have now?

22. Which of the following figures has fewer than 5 faces?

Ⓐ Triangular pyramid

Ⓑ Triangular prism

Ⓒ Cube

Ⓓ Rectangular pyramid

23. Which figure does not have a line of symmetry?

Ⓐ

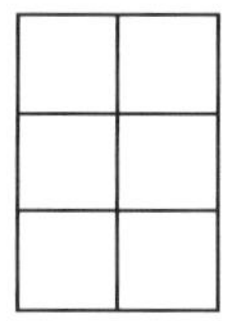

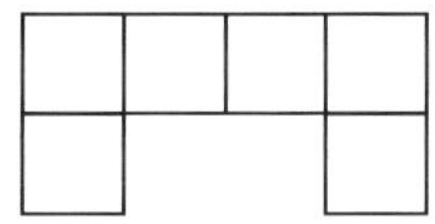

Ⓑ

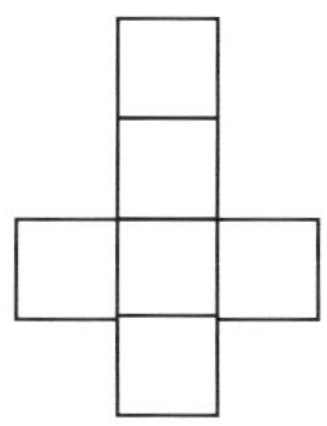

Ⓒ

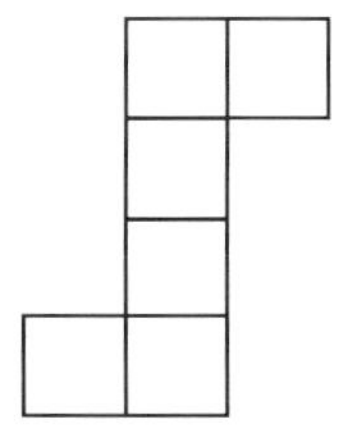

Ⓓ

24. Part A: The figure below is divided into what fraction?

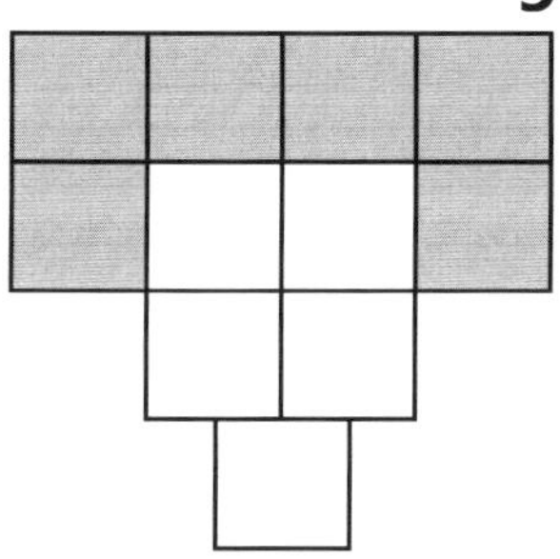

Ⓐ tenths

Ⓑ twelfths

Ⓒ elevenths

Ⓓ thirteenths

Part B: What fraction is shaded in?

Ⓐ $\frac{5}{10}$

Ⓑ $\frac{5}{11}$

Ⓒ $\frac{6}{11}$

Ⓓ $\frac{6}{12}$

25. The rectangle below has an area of 36 sq. cm. What is the length of side *x*?

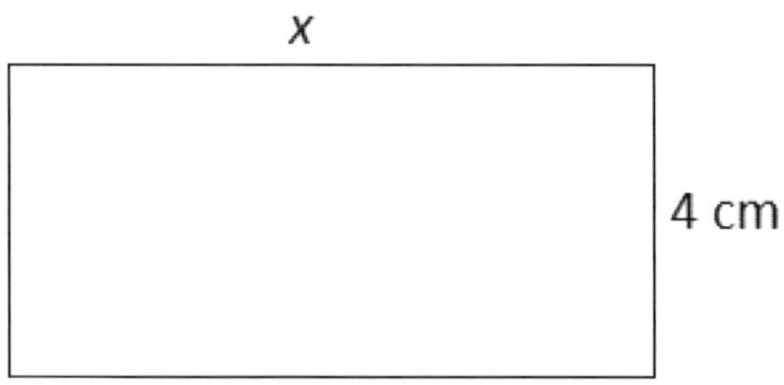

Ⓐ 12 cm

Ⓑ 9 cm

Ⓒ 32 cm

Ⓓ 8 cm

26. What is the perimeter of the pentagon shown below?

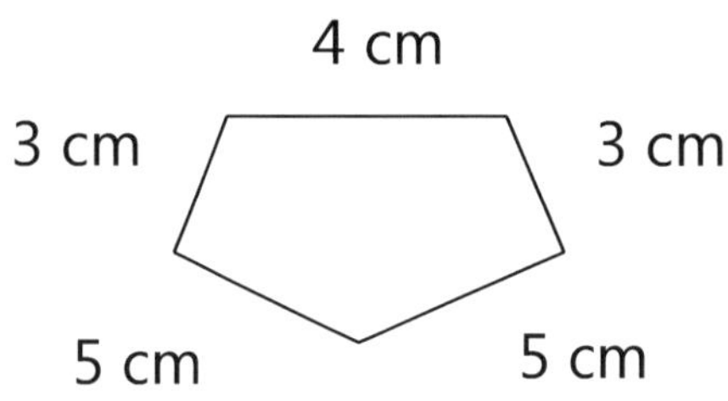

Ⓐ 29 cm

Ⓑ 20 cm

Ⓒ 15 cm

Ⓓ 25 cm

27. A student compares the perimeter of a triangle, a square, a rectangle, and a hexagon. The triangle has side lengths of 3 cm, 5 cm, and 6 cm. The square has a side length of 4 cm. The rectangle has a length of 3 cm and a width of 4 cm. The hexagon has six equal side lengths of 2 cm. Which of these shapes has the largest perimeter?

Ⓐ Triangle

Ⓑ Square

Ⓒ Rectangle

Ⓓ Hexagon

28. Part A: Each day at school Billy spends 30 minutes reading. How many minutes will he read in 6 days?

____

Part B: If each book takes an hour to read, how many books can he read in those 6 days?

____

29. Steve bought 7 watermelons at the store. The total weight of the watermelons was 28 pounds. If each water melon weighed the same amount, how much did one watermelon weigh?

Ⓐ 7 pounds

Ⓑ 4 pounds

Ⓒ 5 pounds

Ⓓ 3 pounds

30. How many square units are found in the shape below?

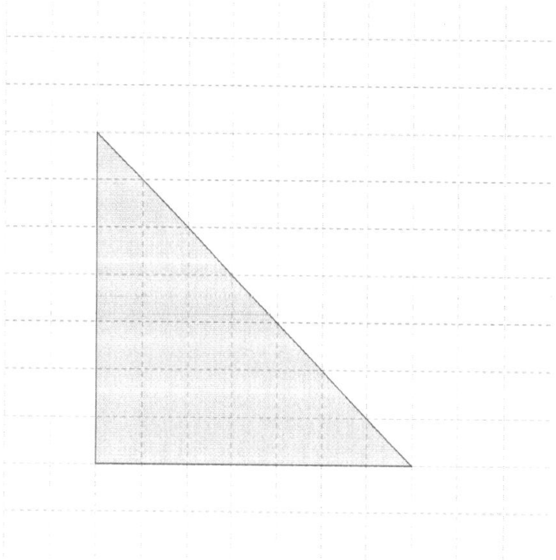

Ⓐ 23 square units

Ⓑ $23\frac{1}{2}$ square units

Ⓒ 24 square units

Ⓓ $24\frac{1}{2}$ square units

31. Part A: A rectangle has a width of 7cm and a length of 9cm. What is its perimeter?

____

Part B: What is the area of the rectangle?

____

32. **John walks from his house to the grocery store in 9 minutes. When he leaves the grocery store it takes him 12 minutes to walk to the dry cleaners. When he leaves there he decides to walk through the park on his way home, and it takes him 23 minutes to get home. How many minutes did John walk from the time he left his house until he returned home?**

Ⓐ 32 minutes

Ⓑ 42 minutes

Ⓒ 44 minutes

Ⓓ 34 minutes

33. **Amanda arrives at a birthday party at the time shown on the clock below.**

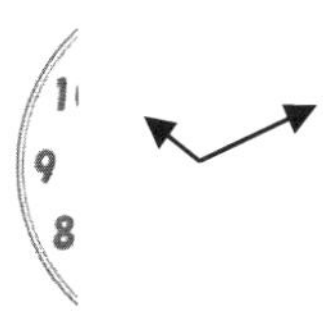

What time did she arrive at the party?

Ⓐ 10:10

Ⓑ 2:10

Ⓒ 9:10

Ⓓ 2:50

34. **A bag contains 3 red cards, 7 blue cards, 9 green cards, and 6 yellow cards. Jesse randomly draws a card from the bag. Which of the following statements is true?**

Ⓐ He is less likely to draw a green card than a yellow card

Ⓑ He is more likely to draw a yellow card than a red card

Ⓒ He is more likely to draw a yellow card than a blue card

Ⓓ He is equally likely to draw a red, blue, green, or yellow card

35. A student spins a spinner, with sections, labeled 1 – 8. Which of the following best represents the likelihood of the spinner landing on a 9?

Ⓐ Likely

Ⓑ Not likely

Ⓒ Certain

Ⓓ Impossible

36. A candy bowl contains 3 chocolates, 7 peppermints, and 4 lollipops. Adeline randomly draws a piece of candy from the bowl. Which of the following statements is true?

Ⓐ She is less likely to draw lollipop than a chocolate

Ⓑ She is more likely to draw a chocolate than a peppermint

Ⓒ She is more likely to draw a peppermint than a lollipop

Ⓓ She is equally likely to draw a chocolate, peppermint, or a lollipop

37. The bar graph below shows the number of Math teachers, from four different states, attending a math event.

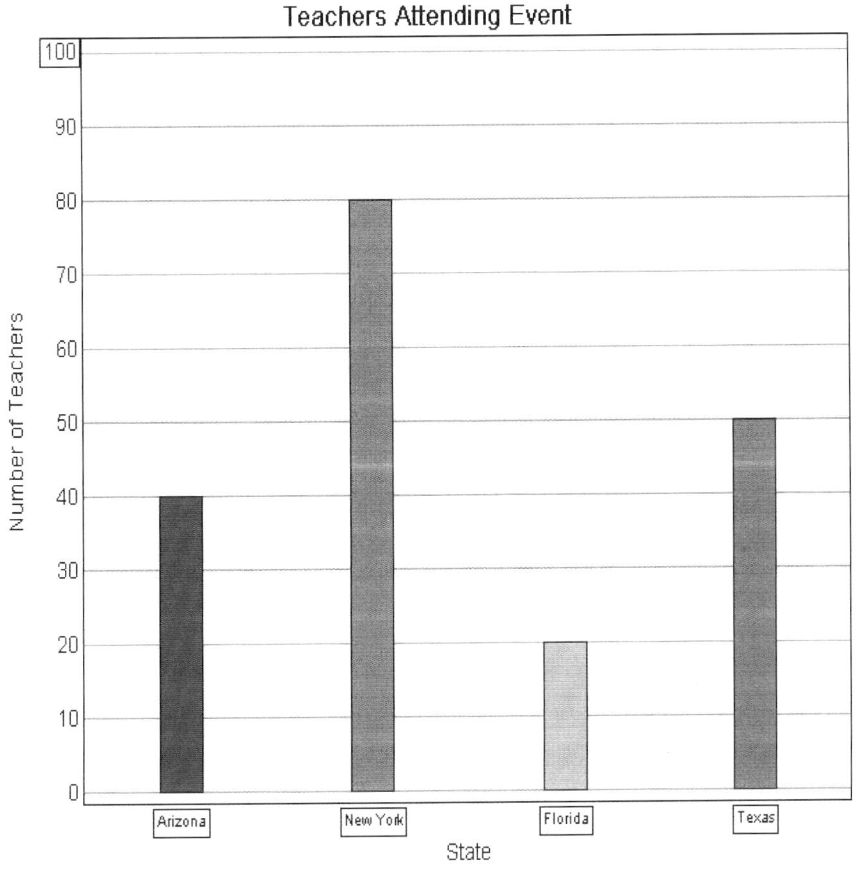

Which state has the fewest number of teachers attending the math event?

Ⓐ Arizona

Ⓑ New York

Ⓒ Florida

Ⓓ Texas

38. The number of cakes baked in one month, by different bakeries, is shown in the table below.

Bakery	Number of Cakes Baked
Bakery A	25
Bakery B	15
Bakery C	35
Bakery D	20

Which pictograph shows the number of cakes baked by each bakery?

Ⓐ 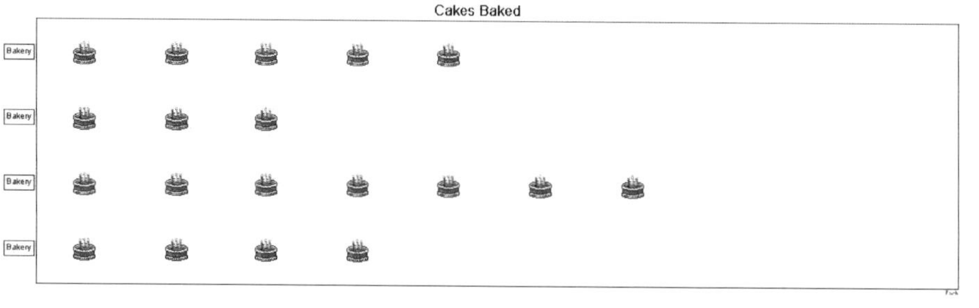

Each picture of a cake represents 5 cakes.

Ⓑ 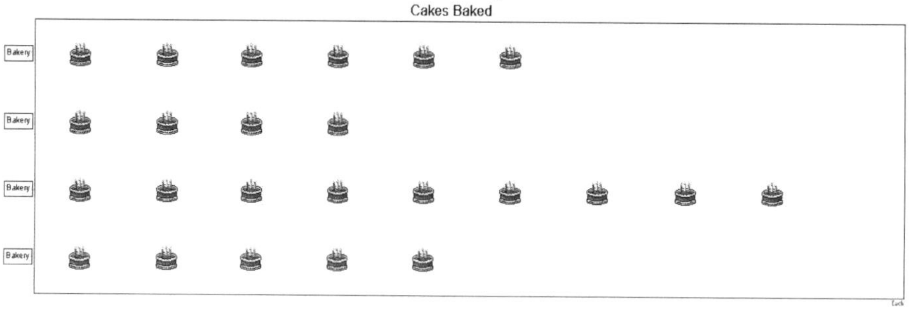

Each picture of a cake represents 4 cakes.

Ⓒ

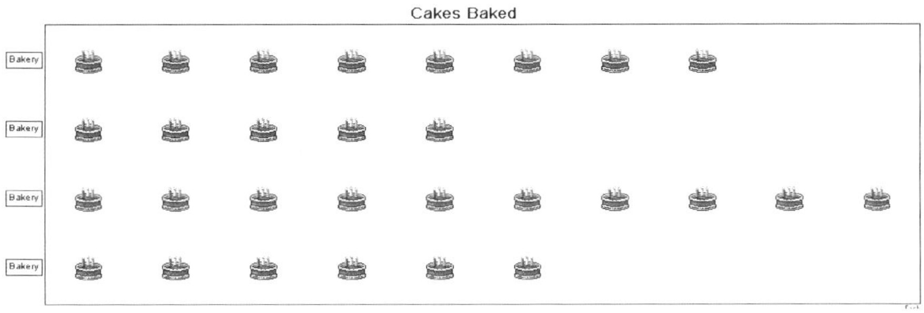

Each picture of a cake represents 3 cakes.

Ⓓ

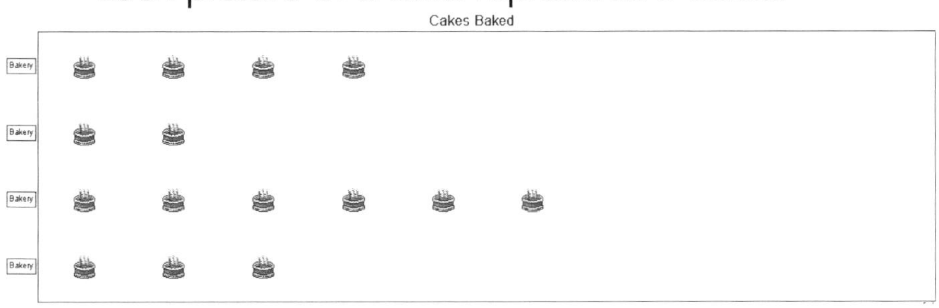

Each picture of a cake represents 6 cakes.

39. The bar graph below shows the number of votes for choosing a class mascot.

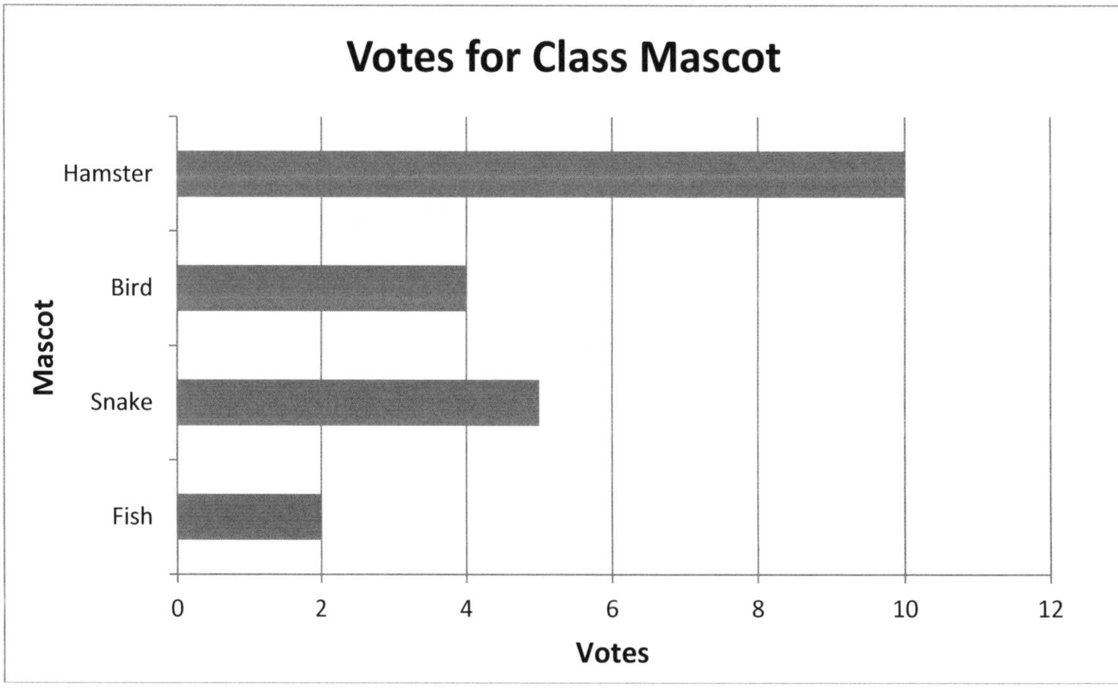

How many more votes did the hamster receive than the fish?

____

40. Which of the following are true? Select all that apply.

I. $4 \times 11 = 40$
II. $32 - 9 = 23$
III. $\frac{4}{5} = \frac{8}{10}$
IV. $7 \times 9 = 61$
V. $\frac{3}{8} = \frac{6}{4}$

Thank You

We at Mometrix would like to extend our heartfelt thanks to you, our friend and patron, for allowing us to play a part in your journey. It is a privilege to serve people from all walks of life who are unified in their commitment to building the best future they can for themselves.

The preparation you devote to these important testing milestones may be the most valuable educational opportunity you have for making a real difference in your life. We encourage you to put your heart into it—that feeling of succeeding, overcoming, and yes, conquering will be well worth the hours you've invested.

We want to hear your story, your struggles and your successes, and if you see any opportunities for us to improve our materials so we can help others even more effectively in the future, please share that with us as well. **The team at Mometrix would be absolutely thrilled to hear from you!** So please, send us an email (support@mometrix.com) and let's stay in touch.

Online Resources

Due to our efforts to try to keep this book to a manageable length, we've created a link that will give you access to all of your online resources:

mometrix.com/resources719/ssncg3mathwb

It's Your Moment, Let's Celebrate It!

Share your story @mometrixtestpreparation

TABLE OF CONTENTS

Workbook Answers

Chapter 1 - Place Value and Number Sense

Pg 6

Pg 7			
No.	**Answer**	**No.**	**Answer**
1	even	13	odd
2	odd	14	even
3	even	15	even
4	even	16	even
5	odd	17	odd
6	even	18	odd
7	odd	19	even
8	odd	20	even
9	even	21	odd
10	odd	22	odd
11	odd	23	even
12	even	24	even

Pg 8		Pg 9		Pg 10		Pg 11	
No.	Answer	No.	Answer	No.	Answer	No.	Answer
1	odd	1	300	1	8,000	1	78
2	even	2	900	2	1,000	2	34
3	even	3	300	3	2,000	3	15
4	odd	4	100	4	9,000	4	2
5	odd	5	200	5	1,000	5	8
6	even	6	800	6	6,000	6	9
7	odd	7	800	7	4,000	7	3
8	even	8	100	8	9,000	8	5
9	even	9	800	9	2,000	9	89
10	even	10	400	10	7,000		
11	odd	11	300	11	2,000		
12	odd	12	300	12	5,000		
13	even	13	600	13	7,000		
14	odd	14	1,000	14	4,000		
15	odd	15	200	15	7,000		
16	even	16	300	16	9,000		
17	even	17	400	17	1,000		
18	even	18	700	18	5,000		
19	even	19	700	19	5,000		
20	even	20	500	20	2,000		
21	odd	21	200	21	2,000		
22	odd	22	800	22	1,000		
23	odd	23	300	23	2,000		
24	even	24	200	24	5,000		
		25	800	25	1,000		
		26	200	26	9,000		
		27	800	27	8,000		
		28	300	28	3,000		

Pg 12		Pg 13		Pg 14	
No.	Answer	No.	Answer	No.	Answer
1	24	1	129	1	1,347
2	43	2	235	2	3,232
3	39	3	254	3	2,459
4	66	4	325	4	4,157
5	59	5	507	5	3,175
6	86				

Pg 15	
No.	**Answer**
1	4,818 | 4,982 | 14,818
2	880 | 1,251 |1,900
3	1,210 | 1,541 | 1,780
4	50 | 74 | 129
5	815 | 1,520 | 3,500
6	3,400 | 5,800 | 9,570
7	10 | 100 | 1,000
8	5 | 300 | 4,500
9	250 | 275 | 300
10	16 | 25 | 54

Pg 16		Pg 17		Pg 18	
No.	**Answer**	**No.**	**Answer**	**No.**	**Answer**
1	>	1	>	1	1,221
2	>	2	<	2	2,142
3	<	3	=	3	333
4	<	4	>	4	3,321
5	<	5	>	5	2,340
6	=	6	>		
7	=	7	<		
8	<	8	<		
9	>	9	=		
10	<	10	<		
11	>	11	>		
12	<	12	<		
13	>	13	>		
14	=	14	=		
15	>	15	<		
16	>	16	<		
17	<	17	=		
18	=	18	>		
19	<	19	>		
20	<	20	<		

Pg 19

The place value of a digit is determined by where it is in a number.

Hundred Thousands	Ten Thousands	Thousands	Hundreds	Tens	Ones
1	2	3	4	5	6

123,456

One Hundred Twenty Three Thousand, Four Hundred Fifty Six

Write these numbers correctly in the blanks.

1. 392,599 =

3	9	2	5	9	9
Hundred Thousands	Ten Thousands	Thousands	Hundreds	Tens	Ones

2. 415,675 =

4	1	5	6	7	5
Hundred Thousands	Ten Thousands	Thousands	Hundreds	Tens	Ones

3. 726,211 =

7	2	6	2	1	1
Hundred Thousands	Ten Thousands	Thousands	Hundreds	Tens	Ones

4. 186,452 =

1	8	6	4	5	2
Hundred Thousands	Ten Thousands	Thousands	Hundreds	Tens	Ones

Chapter 2 – Addition

Pg 21		Pg 22		Pg 23	
No.	**Answer**	**No.**	**Answer**	**No.**	**Answer**
1	79	1	121	1	166
2	89	2	47	2	134
3	62	3	89	3	138
4	77	4	84	4	131
5	99	5	113	5	55
6	106	6	94	6	165
7	78	7	42	7	44
8	38	8	116	8	151
9	69	9	86	9	113
10	78	10	23	10	87
11	29	11	88	11	120
12	47	12	53	12	125
		13	91	13	84
		14	87	14	105
		15	128	15	25
		16	119	16	97
		17	86	17	60
		18	78	18	60
		19	120	19	77

Pg 24	
No.	**Answer**
1	100 + 10 + 10 + 1 = 121
2	100 + 1 + 1 + 1 + 1 + 1 = 105
3	100 + 100 + 100 + 100 + 100 + 10 = 510
4	10 + 10 + 10 + 10 + 1 + 1 = 42
5	100 + 100 + 10 + 10 + 10 + 10 = 240
6	100 + 10 + 1 + 1 + 1 +1 = 114
7	100 + 100 + 100 + 10 + 1 + 1 = 312
8	100 + 10 + 10 + 10 +10 + 1 = 141

Pg 25	
No.	Answer
1	1,000 + 100 + 10 + 1 + 1 = 1,112
2	1,000 + 1,000 + 1,000 + 100 + 1 = 3,101
3	1,000 + 100 + 100 + 10 + 1 + 1 = 1,212
4	1,000 + 1,000 + 1,000 + 1,000 + 100 = 4,100
5	1,000 + 1,000 + 100 + 100 + 10 + 10 = 2,220
6	100 + 10 + 10 + 1 + 1 + 1 = 123
7	1,000 + 1,000 + 100 + 10 + 10 + 1 = 2,121
8	100 + 100 + 100 + 10 + 10 + 1 = 321

Pg 26		Pg 27		Pg 28	
No.	Answer	No.	Answer	No.	Answer
1	1,806	1	1,773	1	2,387
2	892	2	2,782	2	1,190
3	1,330	3	851	3	3,055
4	923	4	1,437	4	2,254
5	1,322	5	1,648	5	1,569
6	831	6	1,286	6	2,266
7	389	7	899	7	1,619
8	1,054	8	1,208	8	2,094
9	1,580	9	2,228	9	1,536
10	204	10	1,511	10	2,321
11	964	11	1,054	11	1,485
12	876	12	1,947	12	1,481
13	1,364	13	1,673	13	1,038
14	648	14	1,395	14	1,833
15	714	15	722	15	1,182
16	1,030				
17	1,046				
18	562				
19	975				

Pg 29

Fill in the blanks to complete each problem.

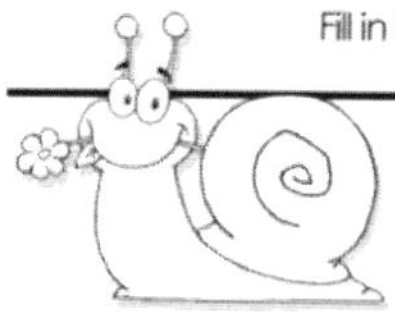

1. 1 2 4 + 1 9 1 = 3 1 5
2. 2 3 9 + 6 3 2 = 8 7 1
3. 3 4 8 + 6 3 1 = 9 7 9
4. 6 2 3 + 2 2 2 = 8 4 5
5. 1 3 7 + 4 4 7 = 5 8 4
6. 5 8 3 + 3 9 1 = 9 7 4
7. 3 7 5 + 1 7 5 = 5 5 0
8. 1 1 5 + 1 2 2 = 2 3 7
9. 4 2 4 + 1 2 3 = 5 4 7
10. 5 2 4 + 2 6 1 = 7 8 5
11. 2 3 4 + 1 6 2 = 3 9 6

Pg 30		Pg 31	
No.	**Answer**	**No.**	**Answer**
1	5,501	1	7,641
2	7,061	2	10,626
3	8,636	3	11,044
4	8,023	4	21,672
5	8,711	5	19,295
6	9,482	6	22,701
7	4,121	7	19,214
8	15,195	8	23,256
9	18,911	9	18,628
10	6,526	10	11,171
11	14,723	11	9,686
12	8,041	12	21,667
13	7,905		
14	10,164		
15	4,399		

Pg 32

- Add the numbers going down
- Add the numbers going across.
- Then add your answers together, either across or down, to fill in the the last square

3	4	7
2	3	5
5	7	12

1.

1	5	6
5	2	7
6	7	13

2.

2	8	10
8	9	17
10	17	27

3.

6	3	9
3	6	9
9	9	18

4.

2	15	17
15	2	17
17	17	34

5.

25	4	29
4	10	14
29	14	43

6.

1	8	9
8	40	48
9	48	57

Pg 33

- Add the numbers going down
- Add the numbers going across.
- Then add your answers together, either across or down, to fill in the the last square

3	4	7
2	3	5
5	7	12

1.

10	3	13
3	10	13
13	13	26

2.

5	8	13
8	5	13
13	13	26

3.

1	7	8
7	1	8
8	8	16

4.

3	6	9
6	12	18
9	18	27

5.

70	13	83
13	45	58
83	58	141

6.

2	36	38
36	2	38
38	38	76

Chapter 3 – Subtraction

Pg 35		Pg 36		Pg 37		Pg 38	
No.	**Answer**	**No.**	**Answer**	**No.**	**Answer**	**No.**	**Answer**
1	13	1	2	1	44	1	28
2	5	2	7	2	45	2	37
3	5	3	7	3	23	3	66
4	36	4	4	4	8	4	42
5	37	5	53	5	23	5	526
6	20	6	61	6	55	6	612
7	22	7	6	7	9	7	523
8	22	8	48	8	8	8	472
9	27	9	68	9	52	9	678
10	14	10	40	10	41	10	378
11	59	11	8	11	33	11	65
12	43	12	60	12	36	12	605
		13	35	13	28	13	341
		14	48	14	61	14	483
		15	17	15	35	15	157
		16	8	16	55	16	77
		17	36	17	2	17	361
		18	31	18	18	18	313
		19	14	19	30	19	87

Pg 39		Pg 40		Pg 41		Pg 42	
No.	**Answer**	**No.**	**Answer**	**No.**	**Answer**	**No.**	**Answer**
1	380	1	182	1	85	1	105
2	658	2	119	2	32	2	80
3	204	3	299	3	136	3	170
4	261	4	106	4	42	4	30
5	457	5	87	5	81	5	135
6	3	6	156	6	53	6	20
7	204	7	155	7	83	7	119
8	277	8	260	8	73	8	199
9	339	9	77	9	112	9	41
10	769	10	110	10	74	10	86
11	359	11	425	11	20	11	50
12	338	12	55	12	61	12	40
13	551	13	208	13	37	13	60
14	249	14	234	14	160	14	15
15	769	15	23	15	40	15	30
16	555	16	236	16	57	16	30
17	520	17	502	17	92	17	187
18	166	18	592	18	16	18	75
19	794	19	104	19	356	19	180
				20	30	20	161

Pg 43		Pg 44		Pg 45		Pg 46	
No.	**Answer**	**No.**	**Answer**	**No.**	**Answer**	**No.**	**Answer**
1	194	1	2,071	1	3,366	1	1,889
2	591	2	2,009	2	904	2	4,267
3	122	3	8,920	3	2,459	3	1,044
4	793	4	2,980	4	154	4	2,589
5	377	5	3,331	5	861	5	3,679
6	881	6	4,091	6	1,248	6	19
7	587	7	5,071	7	3,761	7	889
8	314	8	4,334	8	3,626	8	489
9	233	9	2,781	9	5,071	9	1,175
10	195	10	5,565	10	1,925	10	2,689
11	619	11	7,573	11	2,075	11	1,230
12	214	12	1,121	12	111	12	6,495
13	55	13	1,213	13	3,454	13	3,353
14	66	14	1,151	14	320	14	3,984
15	378						
16	46						
17	473						
18	95						
19	66						

Pg 47	
No.	**Answer**
1	4,690
2	5,844
3	2,045
4	2,571
5	1,784
6	4,222
7	5,406
8	5,897
9	6,122
10	5,009
11	5,329
12	408
13	9,036
14	676

Chapter 4 - Division

Pg 50

Divide the objects equally by the animals for each group.

Objects	Animals	Answer
10 Bananas		5
15 Nuts		3
9 Cheeses		3
14 Bones		7
20 Carrots		5

Pg 51

Divide each group by the numbers in each box and write the answers.

÷ 4 = 2 ÷ 2 = 4	÷ 5 = 2 ÷ 2 = 5
÷ 3 = 4 ÷ 2 = 6	÷ 3 = 5 ÷ 5 = 3
÷ 5 = 4 ÷ 4 = 5 ÷ 2 = 10	÷ 8 = 3 ÷ 4 = 6 ÷ 2 = 12

Pg 52	
No.	Answer
1	18, 9, 2
2	16, 4, 4
3	125, 5, 25
4	15, 3, 5
5	100, 10, 10
6	72, 9, 8
7	4, 12, 3
8	5, 30, 6
9	6, 42, 7
10	8, 64, 8
11	2, 10, 5
12	3, 21, 7

Pg 53		Pg 54		Pg 55	
No.	Answer	No.	Answer	No.	Answer
1	7	1	24 ÷ 8 = 3, 24 ÷ 6 = 4	1	6
2	7	2	15 ÷ 3 = 5, 15 ÷ 5 = 3	2	5
3	46	3	10 ÷ 2 = 5, 10 ÷ 5 = 2	3	6
4	52	4	50 ÷ 5 = 10, 50 ÷ 10 = 5	4	4
5	28			5	4
6	37			6	9
7	27			7	8
8	33			8	9
9	22			9	8
10	99			10	8
11	59				
12	82				
13	80				
14	90				
15	30				
16	97				
17	46				
18	95				
19	59				
20	65				

Pg 56		Pg 57		Pg 58		Pg 59	
No.	**Answer**	**No.**	**Answer**	**No.**	**Answer**	**No.**	**Answer**
1	10	1	20	1	8	1	14
2	4	2	4	2	18	2	5
3	5	3	25	3	10	3	7
4	5	4	15	4	6	4	10
5	7	5	6	5	3	5	7
6	1	6	10	6	4	6	9
7	5	7	5	7	2	7	18
8	10	8	25	8	10	8	10
9	3	9	19	9	7	9	5
10	6	10	12	10	5	10	4
		11	22	11	17	11	36
		12	30	12	6	12	6
		13	10	13	13	13	10
		14	42	14	18	14	36
		15	6	15	21	15	5
		16	18	16	40	16	7
						17	100
						18	10
						19	40
						20	15

Pg 60	
No.	Answer
1	30
2	5
3	63
4	29
5	2
6	7
7	48
8	5
9	4
10	3
11	92
12	9
13	10
14	55
15	6
16	8
17	22
18	7
19	14
20	16

Chapter 5 – Fractions

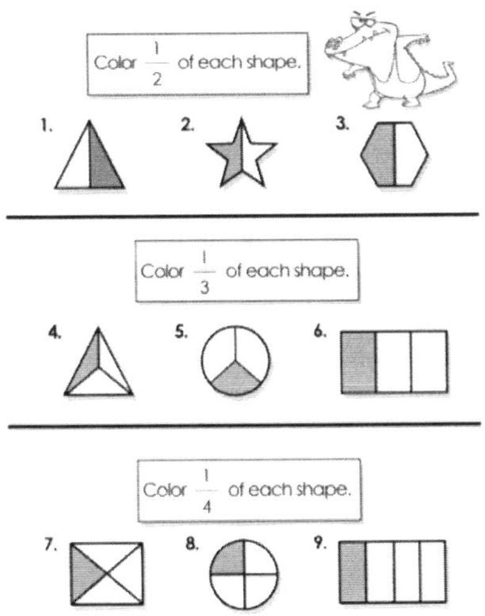

Pg 63

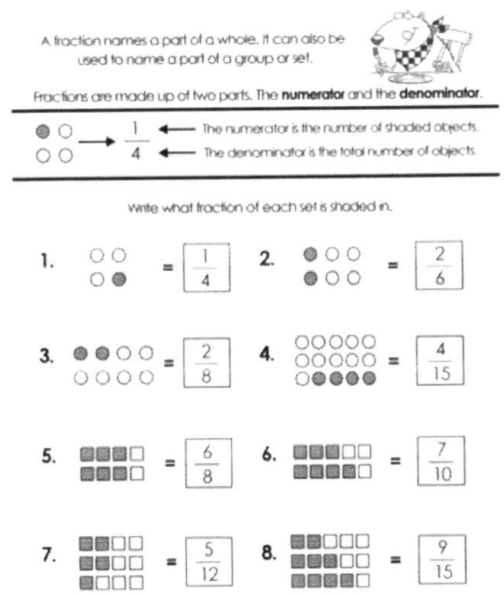

Pg 64

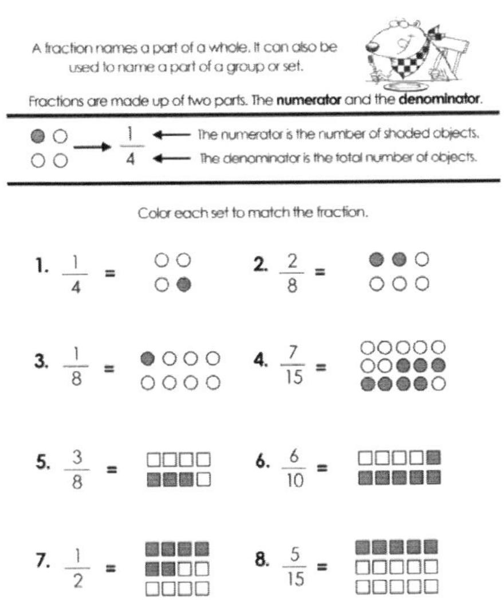

Pg 65

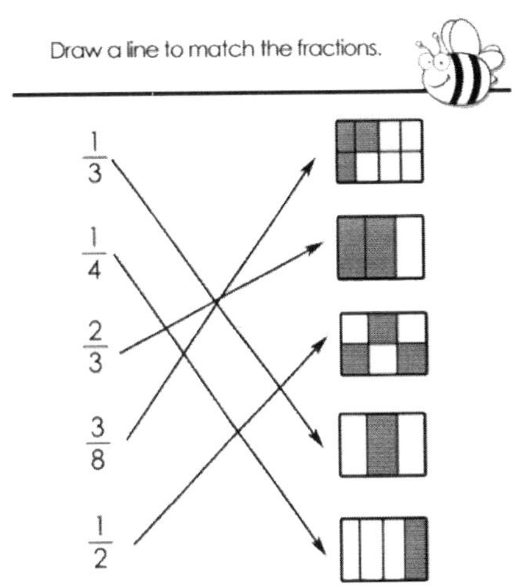

Pg 66

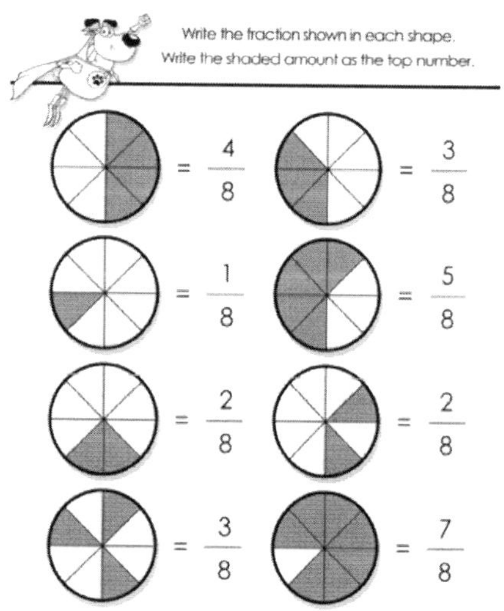

Pg 67

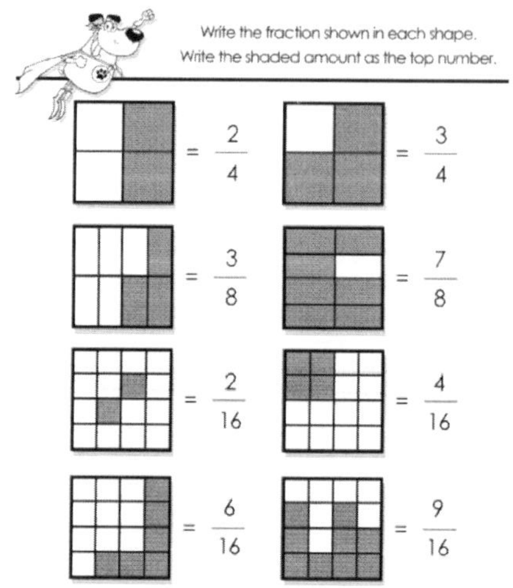

Pg 68

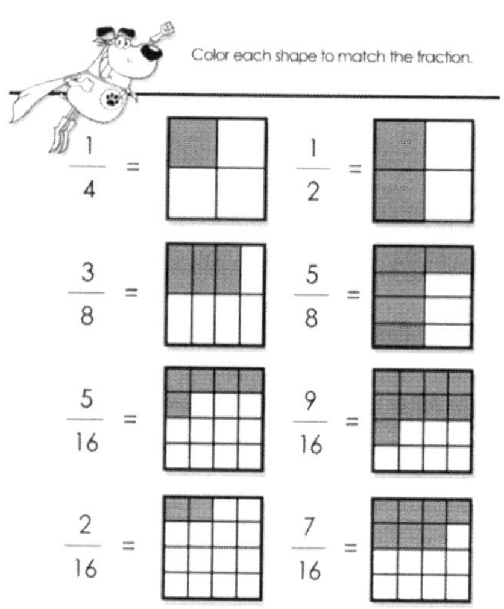

Pg 69

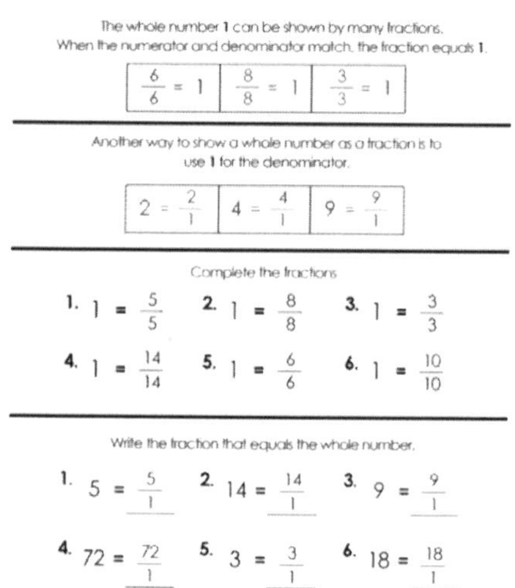

Pg 70

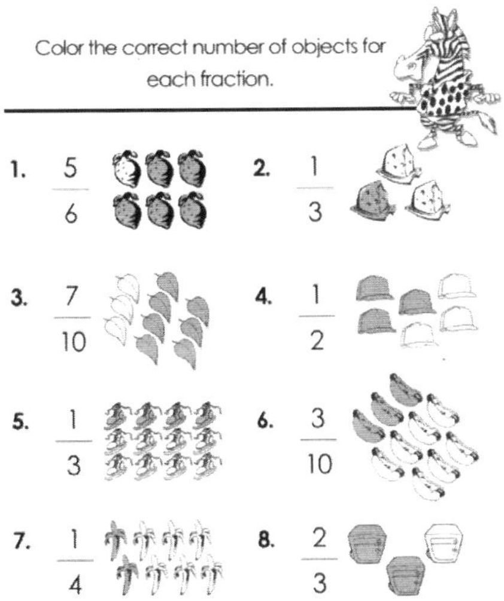

Pg 71

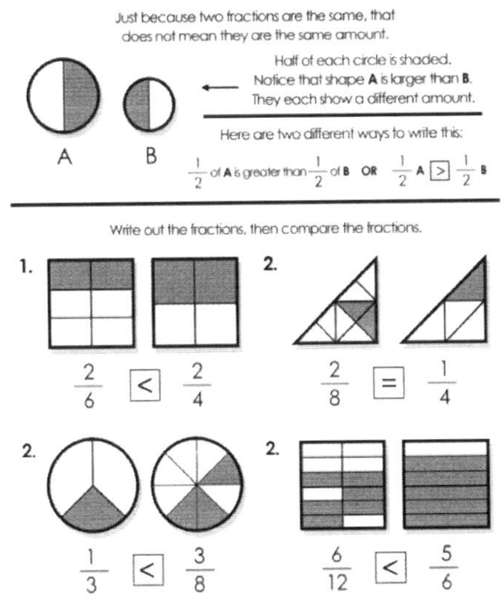

Pg 72

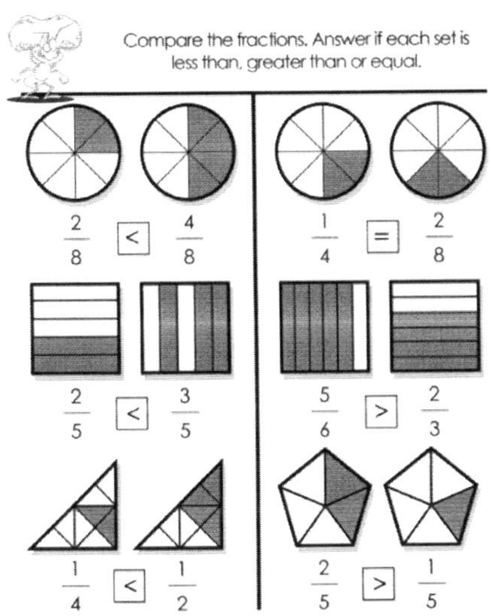

Pg 73

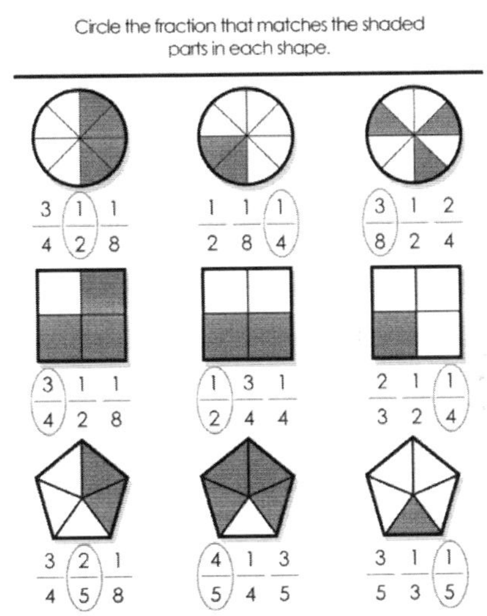

Pg 74

Chapter 6 – Multiplication

Pg 76

Multiplication is the way we find the sum of the same number a certain amount of times.

4 x 2 = 8
2 + 2 + 2 + 2 = 8
□□ □□ □□ □□

2 x 5 = 10
5 + 5 = 10
□□ □□
□□ □□
□ □

Break each group down by writing them out, then adding them together.

1. 3 x 2 = 6
2 + 2 + 2 = 6

2. 3 x 4 = 12
4 + 4 + 4 = 12

3. 4 x 4 = 16
4 + 4 + 4 + 4 = 16

4. 4 x 5 = 20
5 + 5 + 5 + 5 = 20

5. 3 x 8 = 24
8 + 8 + 8 = 24

6. 4 x 10 = 40
10 + 10 + 10 + 10 = 40

5. 2 x 6 = 12
6 + 6 = 12

6. 3 x 6 = 18
6 + 6 + 6 = 18

Pg 77			
No.	**Answer**	**No.**	**Answer**
1	0	12	4
2	4	13	6
3	1	14	5
4	9	15	3
5	9	16	0
6	6	17	2
7	2	18	7
8	8	19	8
9	6	20	7
10	0	21	0
11	3		

Pg 78		Pg 79		Pg 80		Pg 81	
No.	**Answer**	**No.**	**Answer**	**No.**	**Answer**	**No.**	**Answer**
1	18	1	6	1	3	1	12
2	8	2	0	2	0	2	10
3	16	3	4	3	20	3	35
4	7	4	14	4	12	4	18
5	18	5	24	5	4	5	0
6	10	6	12	6	16	6	5
7	7	7	18	7	0	7	18
8	4	8	24	8	28	8	40
9	6	9	0	9	8	9	0
10	6	10	16	10	2	10	16
11	18	11	27	11	36	11	30
12	8	12	21	12	20	12	25
13	14	13	0	13	32	13	4
14	10	14	9	14	4	14	45
15	0	15	2	15	0	15	18
16	12	16	7	16	24	16	16
17	16	17	0	17	18	17	0
18	0	18	15	18	27	18	15
19	4	19	9	19	12	19	9
20	2	20	15	20	12	20	10
21	8	21	18	21	27	21	18

Pg 82		Pg 83		Pg 84		Pg 85	
No.	**Answer**	**No.**	**Answer**	**No.**	**Answer**	**No.**	**Answer**
1	0	1	12	1	56	1	9
2	54	2	0	2	16	2	36
3	15	3	20	3	8	3	56
4	8	4	3	4	12	4	81
5	12	5	42	5	0	5	21
6	6	6	14	6	35	6	40
7	14	7	9	7	72	7	9
8	18	8	21	8	15	8	3
9	36	9	63	9	24	9	24
10	4	10	24	10	0	10	2
11	30	11	28	11	16	11	54
12	24	12	30	12	25	12	16
13	0	13	4	13	16	13	35
14	25	14	35	14	56	14	45
15	27	15	14	15	40	15	36
16	12	16	42	16	72	16	36
17	30	17	7	17	64	17	0
18	15	18	49	18	32	18	18
19	48	19	56	19	32	19	21
20	42	20	7	20	10	20	10
21	0	21	42	21	24	21	27

Pg 86		Pg 87		Pg 88		Pg 89	
No.	**Answer**	**No.**	**Answer**	**No.**	**Answer**	**No.**	**Answer**
1	3	1	30	1	400	1	48
2	4	2	20	2	200	2	219
3	5	3	50	3	500	3	120
4	9	4	60	4	600	4	128
5	6	5	10	5	100	5	48
6	2	6	50	6	400	6	63
7	10	7	40	7	800	7	75
8	8	8	80	8	900	8	108
9	6	9	70	9	0	9	49
10	7	10	0	10	700	10	76
		11	90	11	300		
		12	20	12	700		
		13	40	13	400		
		14	30	14	300		
		15	90	15	900		

Chapter 7 – Graphing

Draw a line on the graph to answer each question.

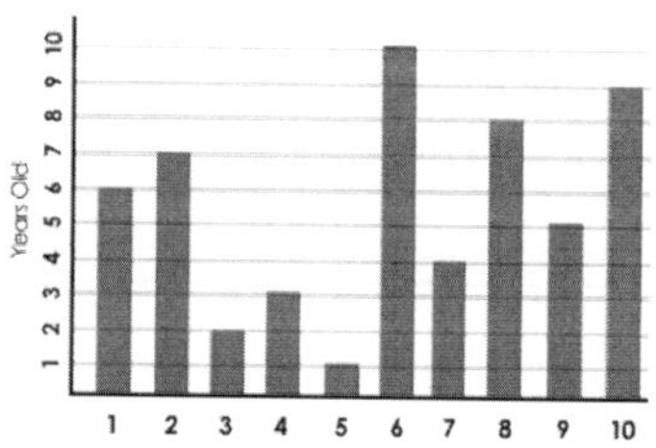

1. Tom is six years old.
2. Laney is seven years old.
3. Jane is two years old.
4. Stan is three years old.
5. Sally is one year old.
6. Mark is ten years old.
7. Mike is four years old.
8. Anne is eight years old.
9. Elle is five years old.
10. Donnie is nine years old.

Pg 91

In the chart below color in the boxes on the graph to show your answers for each question.

1. How many pennies equal a nickel?
2. How many nickels equal a dime?

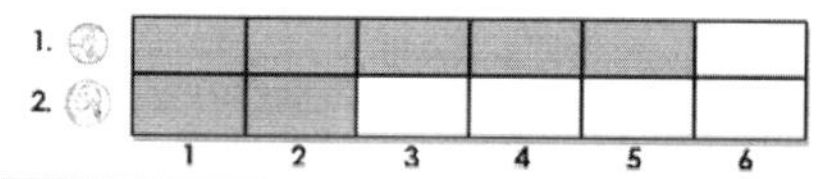

3. How many quarters equal a dollar?
4. How many nickels equal a quarter?

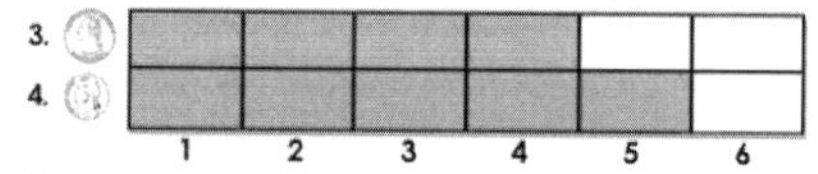

5. How many dimes equal two quarters?
6. How many quarters equal a dollar and a half?

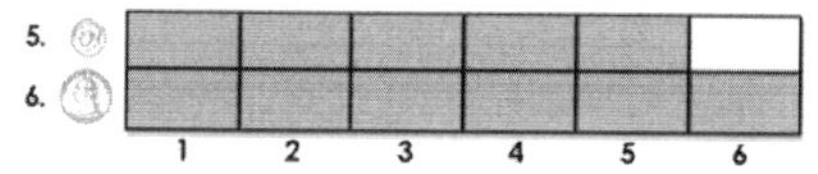

Pg 92

Use the graph to answer the questions.

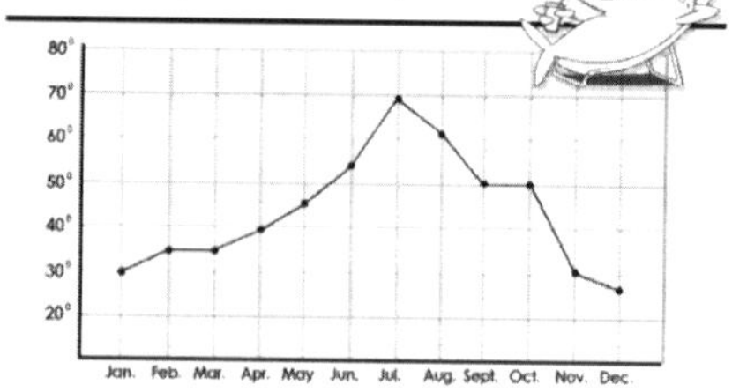

1. What was the coldest month? December
2. What was the hottest month? July
3. What was the temperature in March? 35 degrees
4. About how many degrees was the difference between the coldest and hottest months? 40-45 degrees
5. What was the temperature in November? 30 degrees
6. Did it become hotter or colder from April to May? hotter
7. Did the temperature change from September to October? no
8. Which month was colder, January or December? December

Pg 93

Pg 95	
No.	**Answer**
1	pancakes
2	ham
3	bacon
4	ham
5	bacon
6	pancakes
7	eggs

Pg 96

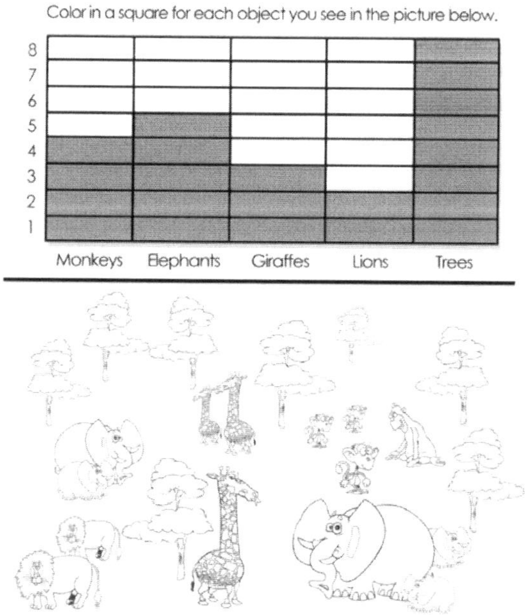

Pg 97		Pg 98	
No.	**Answer**	**No.**	**Answer**
1	3	1	$50
2	5	2	13 miles
3	2	3	32 pieces of candy
4	4	4	97 cupcakes
5	5		
6	1		
7	6		

Pg 99

Locate the points on the grid and draw the shapes for each question.

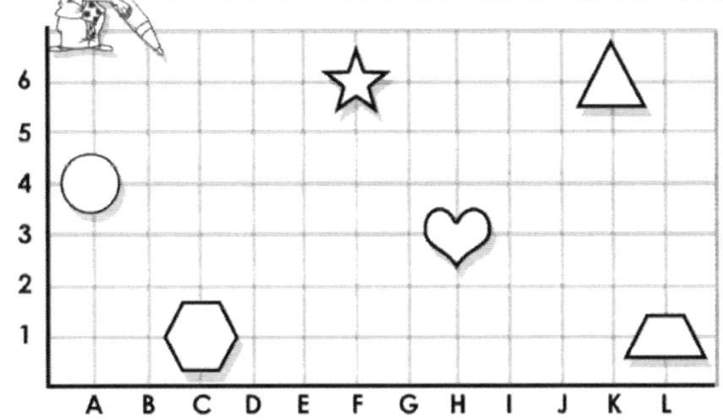

1. A, 4 - 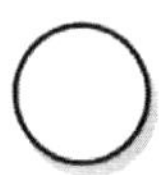

2. C, 1 - 

3. K, 6 - 

4. H, 3 - 

5. F, 6 - 

6. L, 1 - 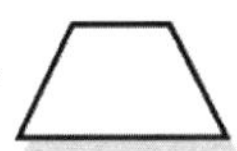

Chapter 8 - Money & Time

Pg 103		Pg 104		Pg 105		Pg 106	
No.	**Answer**	**No.**	**Answer**	**No.**	**Answer**	**No.**	**Answer**
1	76¢	1	$1.41	1	25¢	1	$3.95
2	72¢	2	$3.12	2	23¢	2	$2.39
3	$1.55	3	$7.61	3	36¢	3	$1.68
4	$1.86	4	$30.18	4	52¢	4	$4.39
5	93¢	5	$25.87	5	$3.93	5	$3.91
6	$1.81	6	$35.33	6	$3.64	6	$6.79
7	$1.36			7	$4.36	7	$9.19
8	$1.09					8	$13.20
9	$1.45						

Pg 107	
No.	**Answer**
1	thirty-eight dollars and fifty-nine cents
2	one-hundred dollars and thirty-two cents
3	two-hundred seventy-eight dollars and twelve cents
4	three-hundred fifteen dollars and eight cents
5	nine-hundred fifteen dollars and eighty-three cents
6	eighteen dollars and thirty-three cents
7	two-hundred twenty-nine dollars and twenty-nine cents
8	seven-hundred fifty-six dollars and ten cents
9	six-hundred eighteen dollars and twenty-four cents
10	nine-hundred ninety-nine dollars and seventy-two cents

Pg 109

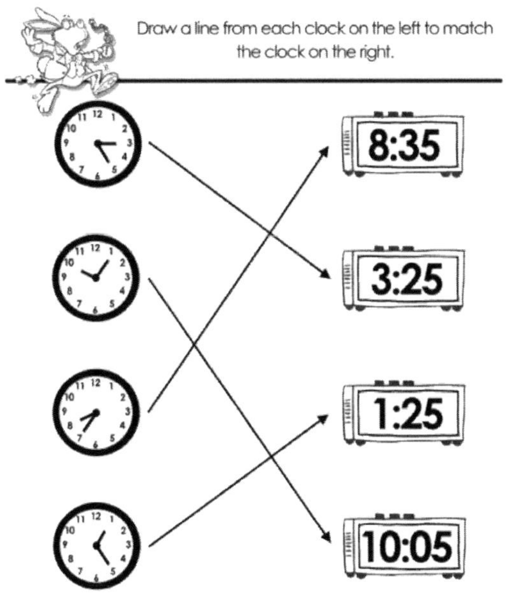

Pg 110		Pg 111	
No.	**Answer**	**No.**	**Answer**
1	AM	1	6 hours 45 minutes
2	PM	2	9 hours 26 minutes
3	AM	3	5 hours 12 minutes
4	PM	4	15 hours 52 minutes
5	PM	5	3 hours 45 minutes
6	AM	6	1 hour 54 minutes
7	PM	7	58 minutes
8	PM	8	3 hours 48 minutes
9	AM		
10	PM		

Pg 112

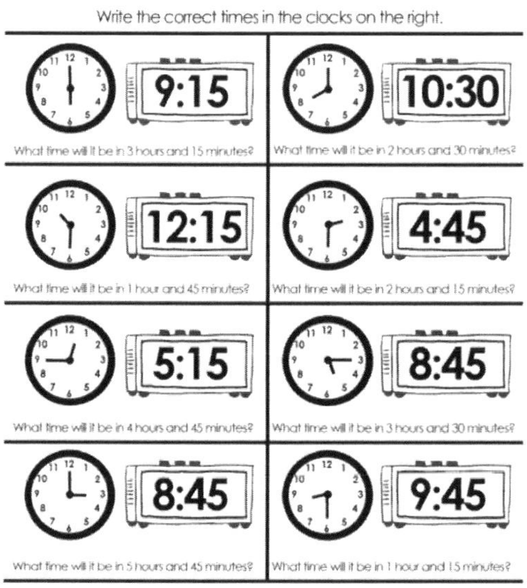
Write the correct times in the clocks on the right.
9:15
What time will it be in 3 hours and 15 minutes?
10:30
What time will it be in 2 hours and 30 minutes?
12:15
What time will it be in 1 hour and 45 minutes?
4:45
What time will it be in 2 hours and 15 minutes?
5:15
What time will it be in 4 hours and 45 minutes?
8:45
What time will it be in 3 hours and 30 minutes?
8:45
What time will it be in 5 hours and 45 minutes?
9:45
What time will it be in 1 hour and 15 minutes?

Pg 113

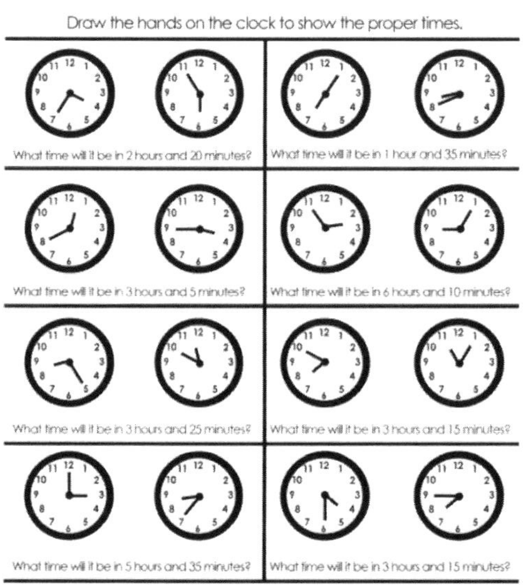
Draw the hands on the clock to show the proper times.
What time will it be in 2 hours and 20 minutes?
What time will it be in 1 hour and 35 minutes?
What time will it be in 3 hours and 5 minutes?
What time will it be in 6 hours and 10 minutes?
What time will it be in 3 hours and 25 minutes?
What time will it be in 3 hours and 15 minutes?
What time will it be in 5 hours and 35 minutes?
What time will it be in 3 hours and 15 minutes?

Chapter 9 - Geometry & Measurements

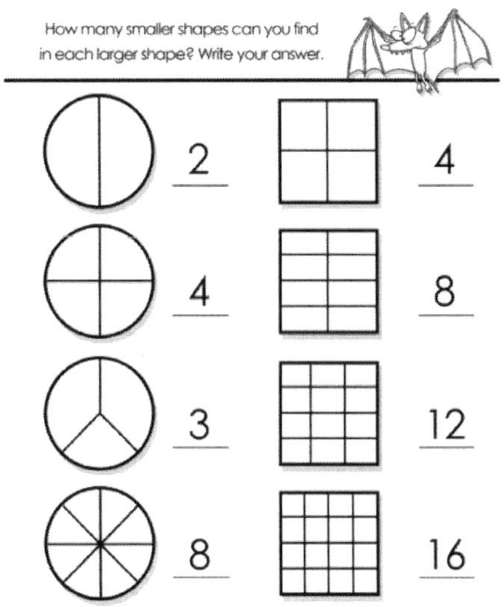

Pg 116

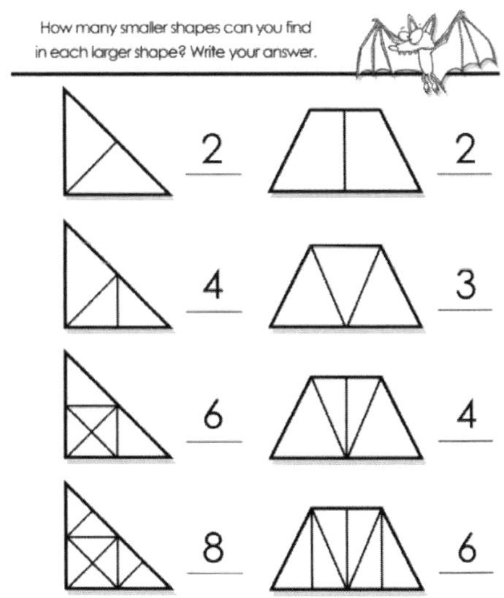

Pg 117

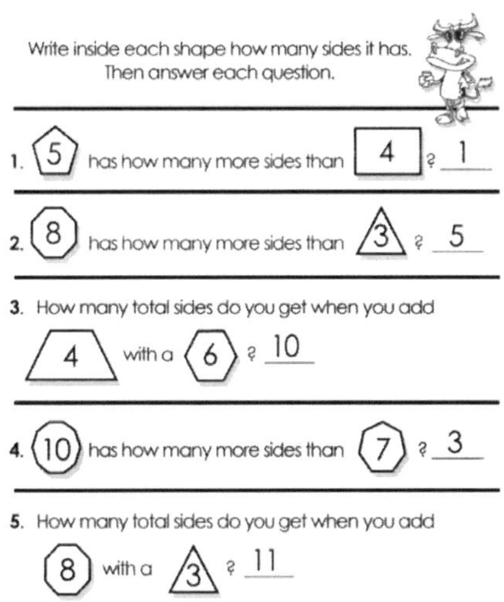

Pg 118

Pg 119	
No.	**Answer**
1	3
2	4
3	6
4	7
5	4
6	7
7	7
8	6

Pg 120

Area is the amount of space inside a shape.

Use the grid to draw the shapes for each question.

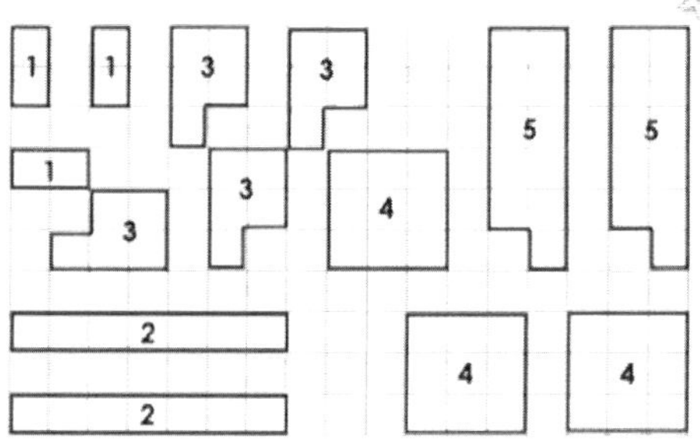

1. Draw 3 shapes with an area of 2 units each.
2. Draw 2 shapes with an area of 7 units each.
3. Draw 4 shapes with an area of 5 units each.
4. Draw 3 shapes with an area of 9 units each.
5. Draw 2 shapes with an area of 11 units each.

Pg 121		Pg 122	
No.	**Answer**	**No.**	**Answer**
1	4 + 6 + 4 +6 = 20 in	1	8
2	7 + 7 + 7 = 21ft	2	10
3	8 + 20 + 20 + 26 = 74in	3	9
4	12 + 8 + 12 + 8 = 40ft	4	12
5	6 + 6 + 9 +6 + 9 = 36in	5	10
6	3 + 3 + 3 + 3 + 3 + 3 = 18ft	6	12
		7	14
		8	14

Pg 123
Answers can vary

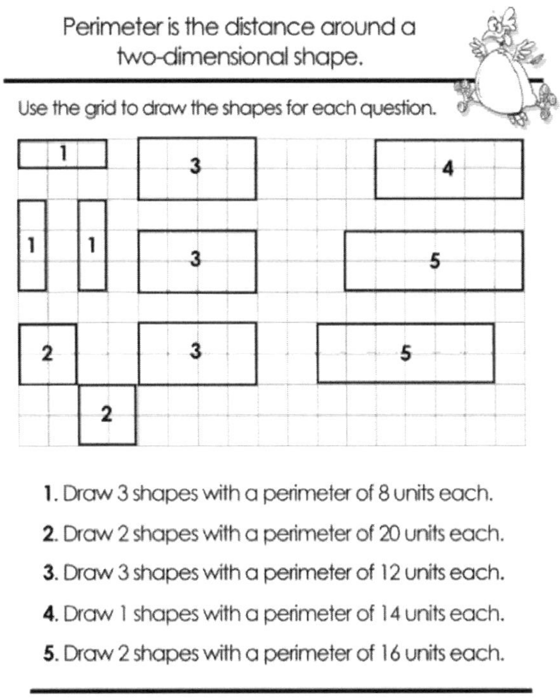
Perimeter is the distance around a two-dimensional shape.

Use the grid to draw the shapes for each question.

1. Draw 3 shapes with a perimeter of 8 units each.
2. Draw 2 shapes with a perimeter of 20 units each.
3. Draw 3 shapes with a perimeter of 12 units each.
4. Draw 1 shapes with a perimeter of 14 units each.
5. Draw 2 shapes with a perimeter of 16 units each.

Pg 124			
No.	**Answer**	**No.**	**Answer**
1	line segment	1	XY or DF
2	point	2	line segment
3	line	3	any point on the illustration
4	line segment	4	line
		5	E

Pg 125		Pg 126		Pg 127		Pg 128	
No.	**Answer**	**No.**	**Answer**	**No.**	**Answer**	**No.**	**Answer**
1	obtuse	1	Ounces	1	yards	1	cup
2	acute	2	Pounds	2	feet	2	gallon
3	right	3	Ounces	3	miles	3	pint
4	obtuse	4	Pounds	4	feet	4	quart
		5	Pounds	5	feet	5	pint
		6	Ounces	6	miles	6	gallon
				7	feet		
				8	yards		
				9	miles		
				10	foot		

Practice Test Answers

Practice Test #1

Answers and Explanations

1. B: The number, 860,002 has an 8 in the hundred-thousands place, a 6 in the ten-thousands place, a 0 in the thousands place, a 0 in the hundreds place, a 0 in the tens place, and a 2 in the ones place. The 860 written in front of the comma represents, "Eight hundred sixty thousand." The 2 in the ones place represents, "Two." Therefore, the number is read, "Eight hundred sixty thousand, two."

2. D: The annual expenses for Years 2009, 2007, 2008, 2011, and 2010 are \$1,046, \$1,224, \$1,319, \$1,342, and \$1,529, respectively. These amounts are listed in order from lowest to highest. Since all of the numbers have a 1 in the thousands place, the numerals in the hundreds place must be compared. For the amounts of \$1,319 and \$1,342, the numerals in the tens place must be compared. No other choice shows the years listed in increasing order of expense.

3. C: There are 2 dollar bills, which represent 2 dollars. There are also 2 quarters, 2 nickels, 1 dime, and 4 pennies. Two quarters are worth \$0.50 since each is worth \$0.25 $(2 \times 0.25 = 0.50)$, 2 nickels are worth \$0.10 since each is worth \$0.05 $(2 \times 0.05 = 0.10)$, 1 dime is worth \$0.10, and 4 pennies are worth \$0.04 since each is worth \$0.01. The sum of the coins can be found by writing: $\$0.50 + \$0.10 + \$0.10 + \$0.04$, which equals \$0.74. The sum of the two dollar bills and the coins can be written as: $\$2.00 + \$0.74$. Thus, he paid \$2.74.

4. B: If 1/3 of the balls Wyatt received were basketballs that means the remaining balls he received must have been soccer balls. Since the fraction used is 1/3, look at it as if he received 3 balls. One ball was a basketball and the remaining balls had to be soccer balls. This is now a simple subtraction problem. 3 - 1 = 2 soccer balls.

5. C: The diagram shows 32 counters divided into 4 groups, with 8 counters in each group. Therefore, the total number of counters, 32, is divided by 4, giving a quotient of 8, which is written as: $32 \div 4 = 8$.

6. I, IV,V: All of these statements can represent 6×5 because they all have 6 groups that contain 5 of something. The other two choices represent $6 + 5$.

7. D: The total number of feet he ascended can be determined by adding 482 feet and 362 feet. The sum of 482 and 362 is 844. Thus, he ascended 844 feet in all.

8. C: The item priced at $4.58 can be rounded to $5. The item priced at $6.22 can be rounded to $6. The item priced at $8.94 can be rounded to $9. The sum of 5, 6 and 9 is 20. Thus, the best estimate is $20.

9. B: Choice B shows 4 shaded sections out of 6 total sections. The fraction, $\frac{4}{6}$, is the same as the fraction, $\frac{2}{3}$. Two shaded sections represent one-third of the total. Thus, four shaded sections represent two-thirds of the total. Each of the pictures has 6 total sections, so the other choices can be written as fractions with a 6 in the denominator. Choice A shows $\frac{3}{6}$, which equals $\frac{1}{2}$. Choice C shows . Choice D shows $\frac{2}{6}$, which equals $\frac{1}{3}$. So, only Choice B shows the correct picture.

10. D: A possible first step would be to divide the number of tiles glued each day by the number of hours it took to glue the tiles. The two quotients would then represent approximately how many tiles glued per hour, and could then be compared.

11. Part A: 96: There are 8 guests at the party that each receives 12 tokens. $8 \times 12 = 96$

Part B: 48: If each game requires 2 tokens to play then the number of games that can be played can be found by dividing the total number of tokens by 2. $96 \div 2 = 48$

12. C: Convert the coins to cents and apply addition. Each nickel is worth 5 cents, so 3 nickels equals 15 cents. Each dime is worth 10 cents, so 4 dimes equals 40 cents. Each penny is worth 1 cent, so 2 pennies equals 2 cents. A quarter is worth 25 cents, so 2 quarters equals 50 cents.. 15 + 40 + 2 + 50 = 107 cents. Since there are 100 cents in a dollar, this becomes 1 dollar with 7 cents remaining or $1.07

13. C: Each figure has 3 more squares than the previous figure, so adding 3 to the number of squares in the previous figure yields the number of squares in the next figure. Thus, he will use 14 squares for Figure 5, 17 squares for Figure 6, 20 squares for Figure7, 23 squares for Figure 8, and 26 squares for Figure 9.

14. C: In order to find the amount donated the following year, you multiply the amount donated the previous year by 3. Thus, the amount donated the second year was $6 ($\$2 \times 3$). The amount donated the third year was $18 ($\$6 \times 3$). The amount donated the fourth year was $54 ($\$18 \times 3$). The amount donated the fifth year was $162 ($\$54 \times 3$).

15. The first answer is 4, because $4 \times 3 = 12$, and this can be found by rearranging the equation to $12 \div 3 = \_\_$. The second answer is 6, because $16 - 6 = 10$, and this can be found by rearranging the equation to $16 - 10 = \_\_$. The last answer is 9, because $8 + 9 = 17$,and this can be found by rearranging the equation to$17 - 8 = __$.

16. D: Each spider has 8 legs. In order to find the number of legs present with 3 spiders, you multiply 3 by 8, which is 24. Thus, 3 spiders have 24 legs in all. Choice D is the only table that shows each number of spiders, multiplied by 8, to yield the correct product representing the total number of legs.

17. C: Each candy jar has 14 pieces of candy. This can be determined by dividing the number of pieces of candy by the number of candy jars: $28 \div 2 = 14, 56 \div 4 = 14, 70 \div 5 = 14, 126 \div 9 = 14$. Since the data in the table shows that there are 14 pieces of candy in each jar, multiplying $13 \times 14 = 182$ finds the total number of pieces of candy that are in 13 candy jars.

18. D: If she drinks 8 glasses of water each day, the number of glasses of water she drinks in 12 days can be determined by multiplying 8 by 12. This product is 96; thus she drinks 96 glasses of water in a 12-day time span. The relationship between the number of glasses of water she drinks per day and the total number of glasses of water she drinks in 12 days can be represented by an appropriate multiplication or division number sentence within the following fact family: $8 \times 12 = 96, 96 \div 8 = 12, 12 \times 8 = 96, 96 \div 12 = 8$. Subtracting 8 from 12 will not reveal the number of glasses she drinks in a 12-day time span. The number sentence: $12 - 8 = ?$, is not in this fact family.

19. The answer should look like:

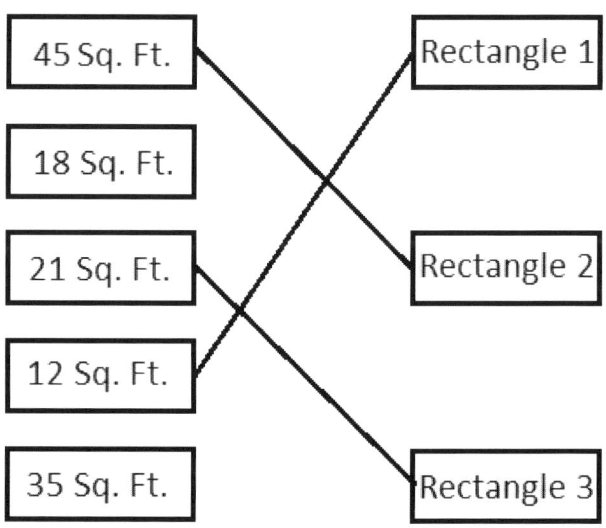

20. D: Choices A, B, and C are all the same right triangle just flipped around. Answer choice D is a different triangle and therefore not congruent.

21. D: 12 ¼ is represented by the first tick mark to the right of the 12. 12 ½ is the second tick mark and 12 ¾ is the third tick mark, or the tick mark before the 13. Only 12 ¾ appears to the right of point M on the number line, making it greater.

22. D: An edge is the intersection of two faces. A triangular pyramid (Choice A) has 6 edges, while a triangular prism (Choice B) has 9 edges, a square pyramid (Choice C) has 8 edges, and a cube (Choice D) has 12 edges. The cube is the only figure with more than 9 edges.

23. C: A vertex is a point where two or more edges meet. A triangle has 3 vertices. Two times that would be 6 vertices. The figure shown for Choice C is a triangular prism, which is the only figure that has 6 vertices. A triangular pyramid (Choice A) has 4 vertices, a cube (Choice B) has 8 vertices, and a square pyramid (Choice D) has 5 vertices.

24. III, V : A face of a shape is each individual surface. Only a cube and a rectangular prism have 6 faces.

25. D: The trapezoid shown for Choice D is congruent to the given shape, provided. Basically, the shapes must be the same size to be congruent, but can be flipped or rotated in any way.

26. Part A: B: Each increment represents one-half. This can be determined by counting that there are 3 marks, or 4 spaces, that lie between the difference of two wholes, as in between 10 and 12. Thus, one increment past 10, where Point P is located, represents $10\frac{1}{2}$.

Part B: A: Point Q is at 9, so the difference between Point P and Point Q is $1\frac{1}{2}$.

27. B: An octagon has 8 lines of symmetry, and 3 lines of symmetry is 5 fewer than 8 lines of symmetry. An equilateral triangle (Choice B) has 3 lines of symmetry, while a square (Choice A) has 4 lines of symmetry, a pentagon (Choice C) has 5 lines of symmetry, and an isosceles trapezoid (Choice D) has 1 line of symmetry. Thus, an equilateral triangle is the only shape shown that has 5 fewer lines of symmetry than an octagon.

28. B: The perimeter is the distance around the figure. So, if you add up all of the numbers you get 22 in.

29. D: The perimeter of the trapezoid is the distance around all of the sides, and is equal to the sum of 3 in, 8 in, 8 in, and 14 in. Thus, the perimeter is 33 in.

30. C: The width of the rectangle is given as 6 in., and the length can be found by multiplying that times 3. $6 \times 3 = 18$

31. C: The trapezoid has 8 square units, plus 4 one-half square units, which equals 2 more square units. The sum of 8 square units and 2 square units is 10 square units.

32. B: The thermometer shows the temperature to be very close to 80 degrees Fahrenheit. It also shows the temperature in Celsius: about 25 degrees.

33. C: The short hand, or hour hand, is between 6 o'clock and 7 o'clock, revealing that Karen went to the library after 6 o'clock. The long hand, or minute hand, is pointed at the 2. Since the 2 on the clock represents 10 minutes after the hour (since each number shown on the clock represents 5 minutes and $2 \times 5 = 10$), the clock shows that Karen went to the library at 6:10.

34. B: There are 16 small squares in total. This means that for $\frac{5}{8}$ of them to be shaded there would need to be 10 of them shaded.

35. 27: To find out how long it takes Ashley to get ready just add up all of the minutes that she spends doing various activities. $6 + 7 + 12 + 2 = 27$

36. D: Texas has the most zoos because it has 15 zoos, while the other states each have 7 zoos, 4 zoos, and 11 zoos. Also, it can be seen from the graph that the bar representing Texas is much higher than the bars for the other states.

37. D: The more fish there is of a certain color the more likely it is that the color of fish is scooped. With more orange fish than striped fish in the bowl, he is more likely to scoop an orange fish than a striped one. There are equal amounts of striped and blue fish, so one is not more likely than the other. There are more orange fish than blue fish, so he is more likely to scoop an orange fish than a blue one.. Finally, the number of striped and blue fish is the same - so they are equally likely to be scooped compared to each other. Thus, Choice D is the only true statement.

38. D: This answer just breaks down the first equation. It adds all of the 10's places first, then adds all of the 1's places.

39. C: Baseball received 6 votes and basketball received only 2 votes. The difference is 6 - 2 = 4 fewer votes.

40. A: Since each tree represents 2 lawns, the pictograph shows that the number of lawns finished by Company A is equal to 6×2, or 12 lawns, the number of lawns finished by Company B is equal to 9×2, or 18 lawns, the number of lawns finished by Company C is equal to 3×2, or 6 lawns, and the number of lawns finished by Company D is equal to 8×2, or 16 lawns. This is the only pictograph that represents the correct number of lawns.

Practice Test #2

Answers and Explanations

1. C: The term subtracted from means to "take away" and place a minus sign in the equation. Since 5 is being subtracted from 25, write the number 25 first followed by a minus sign and then the number 5. The problem states that this subtraction equals 5, so simply attach this to the end.

2. D: Choice D shows 1 crayon and 3 pencils, indicating that 1 out of 4 of Camille's writing tools were crayons. The other choices are out of either a total of 7 writing tools or 5 writing tools, which cannot be used in a ratio that represents 1 out of 4.

3. D: In order to find out the total number of hot dogs she sold in the two months, the amount sold in each month should be added. The sum of 128 and 117 is 245. Thus, she sold 245 hot dogs during the two months.

4. D: The diagram shows 24 counters total, divided into 3 groups, with 8 counters in each group. Therefore, the total number of counters, 24, is divided by 3. This gives a quotient of 8, which is written as: $24 \div 3 = 8$.

5. I, II, V: $2 \times 3 = 6$, so that makes that I. the same. II and V are both 6 groups of 8, which is the same as 6×8.

6. The first on is 4. To find this rearrange the equation to $28 \div 7 = 4$. The second one is 13. To find this rearrange the equation to $22 - 9 = 13$. The last one is 13. To find this rearrange the equation to $18 - 5 = 13$.

7. A: Since a chicken has 2 feet and a horse has 4 feet, you may multiply the number of chickens found on each farm by 2, and then multiply the number of horses found on each farm by 4. After finding the total number of chicken feet and horse feet on each farm, you can then add the two amounts to find the total number of animal feet on each farm. You can then compare the two values to determine the one that is larger.

8. B: Each model shows a whole, split into 7 sections. This makes the denominator equal to 7 for the fraction representing the shaded section for each. Since the fractions all have the same number on the bottom, the number of shaded sections can be compared. For a fraction to be more than $\frac{4}{7}$, more than 4 parts must be shaded. The model shown for Choice B shows the fraction $\frac{6}{7}$, because 6 out of 7 sections are shaded, showing a fraction that is more than 4 out of 7. The other choices all show either 4 parts or less than 4 parts shaded.

9. B: The sequence of the number of miles walked in order from greatest to least is: 963 (Year 4), 691 (Year 1), 567 (Year 2), 221 (Year 5), 144 (Year 3). The number of miles walked can also be compared by examining only the digits in the hundreds place since they are all different. 9 is greater than 6 which is greater than 5 and so on. The only choice that shows the years for the number of miles walked in descending order is B.

10. D: 23 + 12 + 34 = 69. Since the 9 in the ones digit is greater than or equal to five, the number is rounded up to 70.

11.I and IV: To find the answer reduce the fractions to their lowest terms. For the first one, $\frac{4}{6}$, both the numerator and denominator can be divided by 2 to get $\frac{2}{3}$. For the fourth one, $\frac{10}{15}$, both the numerator and the denominator can be divided by 5 to get $\frac{2}{3}$.

12. II and III: To figure out which one is bigger first you need to find a common denominator. The least common denominator of 6 and 8 is 24. So, convert $\frac{5}{8}$ to $\frac{15}{24}$, and $\frac{5}{6}$ to $\frac{20}{24}$, and you see that $\frac{5}{6}$ is bigger. The $\frac{3}{4}$ can just be converted to $\frac{6}{8}$, and you can see that it is bigger than $\frac{5}{8}$.

13. B: The farmer plants 17 rows of corn each season. This can be found using all of the information given in the table. The farmer had planted 34 rows of corn by the end of Season 2 and 68 rows of corn by the end of Season 4, indicating an increase of 34 rows of corn between the two seasons. So, by dividing 34 by 2, the numbers of rows planted in one season is found. Also, the farmer had planted 102 rows of corn by the end of Season 6 and 119 rows of corn by the end of Season 7, indicating an increase of 17 rows of corn planted in one season. If 17 rows of corn are added to the number given at the end of Season 2, the result is 51 rows of corn planted by the end of Season 3. If another 17 rows of corn are added to this amount, the farmer would have planted 68 ears of corn by the end of Season 4, which he did. Thus, he did plant 17 rows of corn each year. He had planted 136 rows of corn by the end of Season 8, 153 rows of corn by the end of Season 9, and 170 rows of corn by the end of Season 10.

14. 35 cm: To find the area of a rectangle just multiply the length times the width.

15. B: A number sentence that subtracts the number of friends from the total number of stamps will not provide the number of stamps needed to give each friend. Instead, an appropriate multiplication or division number sentence within the following fact family is needed: $9 \times 5 = 45$, $5 \times 9 = 45$, $45 \div 9 = 5$, or $45 \div 5 = 9$.

16. D: The number of books brought by 2 students is 8, while the number of books brought by 5 students and 6 students increased by 4. Thus, the number of books brought by each student was 4. This fact can be checked by starting with 1 student and 4 books brought, and continuing the pattern to make sure it corresponds with the numbers in the table. For example, 8 students brought 32, which does in fact agree with the each student bringing 4 books. So, the number of books each student brought, 4, is multiplied by the number of students to find the total number of books that were brought. Thus, 12 students brought 12×4 books, or 48 books.

17. A: A vertex is a point where two or more edges meet. So, a triangular prism (Choice A) has 6 vertices, while a square pyramid (Choice B) has 5 vertices, a triangular pyramid (Choice C) has 4 vertices, and a cube (Choice D) has 8 vertices. Thus, the triangular prism is the only figure with 6 vertices.

18. D: A line of symmetry is a line that can be drawn through a shape such that the remaining part of the shape on either side of the line looks the same, but is reflected. The shape shown is a hexagon, and it has 6 lines of symmetry. An octagon (Choice D) has 8 lines of symmetry, while an equilateral triangle (Choice A) has 3 lines of symmetry, a rhombus (Choice B) has 2 lines of symmetry, and a trapezoid (Choice C) has 1 line of symmetry. So, the only shape with more lines of symmetry than the hexagon is the octagon.

19. Each tick mark on the number line represents a change of $\frac{1}{4}$. The number line below shows the correct placement of the point.

20. B: The figure shown is a square pyramid. It indeed has 5 vertices and 5 faces. It has 8 edges, not 6 edges, so Choice B is the only statement that is not true.

21. 185: She starts with 152 stickers and then gives 34 away. So, 152-34=118. Then she buys 67 more, which gives her 118+67=185.

22. A: A triangular pyramid (Choice A) has 4 faces, while a triangular prism (Choice B) and a rectangular pyramid (Choice D) both have 5 faces. A cube (Choice C) has 6 faces. Thus, the only figure with less than 5 faces is the triangular pyramid.

23. D: Figures A, B, and C can all be folded in a manner that the squares lay directly on top of each other. This cannot be done with Figure D; therefore, Figure D does not have a line of symmetry.

24. Part A: C: If you count all of the boxes you see that the figure is divided into 11 pieces.

Part B: C: Now count the boxes that are shaded in and you get 6, so $\frac{6}{11}$ are shaded.

25. B: The area of a rectangle is found by multiplying length times width. In this problem you are given the area and the width and asked to find length *x*. To find this divide 36 by 4 to get 9.

26. B: The perimeter is the sum of the lengths of all five sides, or $5 + 5 + 3 + 3 + 4$, which equals 20. Therefore, the perimeter of the pentagon is 20 cm.

27. B: To find the perimeter of each shape, add up the lengths of all of the sides. The square has four sides of equal length, so it has a perimeter of 16 centimeters, which is larger than the perimeters of the other three shapes. The triangle and rectangle each have a perimeter of 14 centimeters. The hexagon has a perimeter of 12 centimeters.

28. Part A: 180: To find the total number of minutes he reads multiply 6 times 30 to get 180.

Part B: 3: An hour is 60 minutes, so if takes 180 and divide by 60 to get 3.

29. B: The total weight of the watermelons was 28, and if each one weighed the same then you can just divide by 7 to get 4 pounds each.

30. D: The triangle includes 21 whole square units, plus 7 one-half square units, or $3\frac{1}{2}$ square units. So, 21 square units plus $3\frac{1}{2}$ square units gives a total of $24\frac{1}{2}$ square units.

31. Part A: 32cm: The perimeter of a rectangle is the length of all of the sides added together. The length is 9 and the width is 7, but there are two lengths and two widths, so $7 + 7 + 9 + 9 = 32$ cm.

Part B: 63 cm: The area of a rectangle id length times width, so $7 \times 9 = 63$.

32. C: To find how much total time John spent walking, add the time together. 9 minutes plus 12 minutes plus 23 minutes equals 44 minutes, $9 + 12 + 23 = 44$. Therefore, John walked for a total of 44 minutes from the time he left his house until he returned home.

33. A: The short hand, or hour hand, is between 10 o'clock and 11 o'clock, revealing that Amanda arrived after 10 o'clock, but before 11 o'clock. It is much closer to the 10, so this indicates the time is much closer to 10 o'clock than 11 o'clock. The long hand, or minute hand, is pointing to the 2, indicating 10 minutes after the hour. This is because for minutes, each number represents 5 minutes; so $2 \times 5 = 10$. So, she arrived at the party at 10:10.

34. B: There are 6 yellow cards and 3 red cards. The more cards there are of a certain color, the more likely it is that the color is drawn. With more yellow cards than red cards in the bag, he is more likely to draw a yellow card than a red card. There are more green cards than yellow cards, so he is more likely to draw a green card than a yellow card. There are less yellow cards than blue cards, so he is less likely to draw a yellow card than a blue card. Finally, the number of red, blue, green, and yellow cards are all different - so none of them are equally likely to be drawn compared to another color. Thus, Choice B is the only true statement.

35. D: Since the spinner only has sections, labeled 1 - 8, there is not a section, labeled "9". Therefore, it is impossible for the spinner to land on a 9.

36. C: The more candy there is of a certain kind, the more likely it is that the candy is drawn. With more lollipops than chocolates in the bowl, she is more likely to draw a lollipop than a chocolate. There are more peppermints than chocolates, so she is more likely to draw a peppermint than a chocolate. There are more peppermints than lollipops, so she is more likely to draw a peppermint than a lollipop. Finally, the number of chocolates, peppermints, and lollipops are all different - so none of them are equally likely to be drawn compared to another color. Thus, Choice C is the only true statement.

37. C: Florida had 20 teachers that attended the event, which is less than the number of teachers who attended the event from each of the other three states. The number of teachers that attended the event from each of the other states were 40 (Arizona), 80 (New York), and 50 (California). Also, just looking at the bar graph shows that Florida had the least number of teachers attend compared to the other states because the bar is much lower in the graph.

38. A: The pictograph for Choice A reveals that each picture of a cake represents 5 actual cakes. Therefore, the numbers given in the table, divided by 5, should equal the number of cakes represented in the pictograph. The pictograph accurately shows 5 cakes for 25 actual cakes, 3 cakes for 15 actual cakes, 7 cakes for 35 actual cakes, and 4 cakes for 20 actual cakes. This is the only pictograph that represents the correct number of cakes.

39. The hamster received 10 votes and the fish received 2 votes. The difference is 10 - 2 = **8 votes**.

40. II and III: $32 - 9 = 23$ is a true statement. Also $\frac{4}{5} = \frac{8}{10}$ is true because 4 and 5 can each be multiplied by 2 to get 8 and 10.

Online Resources

Due to our efforts to try to keep this book to a manageable length, we've created a link that will give you access to all of your online resources:

mometrix.com/resources719/ssncg3mathwb

It's Your Moment, Let's Celebrate It!

Share your story @mometrixtestpreparation